Our Stories
MATTER
Rev. William R. Grimbol

Orange Hat Publishing
www.orangehatpublishing.com - Waukesha, WI

This book is dedicated to one dream of a lady, Sandy Carlson Tarlow. She brought to life a rare devotion to beauty, a simple elegance of style, and a remarkable capacity to inspire.

Sandy was also a truly gifted mother, and helped raise a son who will always reflect her magical soul and maverick spirit.

Sandy had a dream her death threatens to extinguish. She wanted to enable youth to tell their stories, declare their dreams, plan and actualize their hopes, and become genuine creative forces in this world. It is my hope this manuscript will help keep her dream aloft.

Sandy was never a dimly burning wick, but a true torch. Long may she blaze — perhaps, for an eternity.

FOREWORD

Sandy Carlson and I were never what I would call, close friends. Our relationship was, however, deep, intimate, and quite mature – even spiritual. I believe we respected and admired one another, and very much enjoyed each other's company – insights, acerbic wit, and refreshing candor.

We first met over lunch at the Paradise Café in Sag Harbor. She was stunning to look at, and had a Bacall voice. She had called me over concern for her teenage son Cody, who had gone to a school dance at Collegiate, a posh private prep school in NYC, in drag. She needed to discuss her response.

We first chatted about the predicted storm coming that weekend, and shared bits of Shelter Island trivia, but then Sandy cut to the chase, and asked, "Well, tell me what you think about Cody's behavior, and if I have something to be concerned about?"

"Did his shoes match his purse?" I calmly asked.

After several seconds of silence, a smile sprouted on her face, and we both erupted in laughter.

"Sandy, I certainly do not know Cody well, but I do know he is a bright and very gifted young man, and that he is not a big fan of authority or the status quo."

"Is that a good thing?" she asked as a Mom.

"It is exactly who you and Dick raised him to be."

"True," she said with renewed composure and relief.

"I doubt you need to impose any consequences on Cody. He will choose to handle it his own way. There may be some fallout of course, but I doubt much, and I would chalk this up as just one of the many times when Cody will be true to his calling to be a rebel with a cause."

"Let's eat," she said in a voice which displayed renewed pride.

It would be several months later when Sandy called to ask me for a return lunch at the Paradise. I asked her if Cody was still wearing fishnets, and she told me he had entered a decidedly heterosexual phase which was just as alarming. Again, we laughed.

After ordering she launched into telling me a dream of hers – which left me dumbstruck.

Sandy told me that she was ready to retire. I don't believe she knew I hadn't a clue about her work for Ralph Lauren, or her being the vision behind the magnificent Polo advertising brand. She said that after twenty-seven years, she had managed to create advertising which spoke for itself – people would know it was a Polo ad without even hearing the name. I agreed.

She then stunned me by sharing her desire to create a spiritual retreat center for youth on Shelter Island. She was clear in hoping for my involvement and support, but also adamant in her belief the Center must not be focused on teen problems. She had made her point. I was often too caught up in the chaos of teen angst, and what she was hoping to create was a place and people devoted to helping youth launch their dreams – a creative sanctuary of a kind.

She next said she wanted to host a couple of dinners at her Shelter Island home, and that I was to provide the young women, while she would choose a panel of accomplished women to speak – not all of whom would be wealthy. She had clearly thought this through, and it bore her signature style. She already had the menu, a must when talking with teens.

I got a dozen plus young women. Sandy brought in a wonderful cast of ladies, some from NYC and some from Shelter Island. The women shared their stories of trying to make their dreams come true. The stories were splendid and featured failures and flops and flaws, and the magnificent rewards of fulfillment. The young girls got to ask scads of questions – and did.

After dinner, the young girls were invited to share their dreams. It was remarkable. Once given the opportunity, I witnessed my youth group females speak with passion and authority and hope and drive and a seemingly boundless energy. The adults were blown away. We all commented on how impressed we were. The young women told us they had never been asked before.

Sandy was delighted. She held another dinner, and had an equally positive and productive result. We planned two more for late in autumn. But – it was then that Sandy was tragically diagnosed with lung cancer; to which she would succumb mere months later. The loss was huge and heartbreaking.

Her funeral was a most memorable event, one of great joy and deep satisfaction, with each speaker capturing a facet of her gracious and generous soul. Before heading in to lead the service, Cody gave me a hug and told me to "go get them Pastor Bill", which was his classic way of telling me to tell the gospel truth but keep the religious crap away. He had indeed become exactly who she had raised him to be.

Over the years since Sandy's passing, I have often thought of her dream. It has been a pleasant haunting of a kind. Now retired, I have returned to it, and offer this manuscript as one practical way of fleshing out Sandy's dream. Though I take full credit for the book's content, it was Sandy's voice and vision which first called it forth.

I am indebted to Sandy, and it is my profound hope this book honors the memory of one lovely lady who knew what kids in America truly needed – mature adults who would help them launch their dreams. By the way, she called her idea DREAM BY DESIGN, and this manuscript offers my design for helping our youth find those stories which might ignite their dreams, and inspire them to make them come true.

Quote Workbook

"Stories, like whiskey, must be allowed to mature in the cask."
— Sean O'Faolain, Atlantic Monthly, 1956

"The color of truth is gray."
— Andre Gide

"Of course, it's the same old story.
Truth usually is the same old story."
— Margaret Thatcher

"I can find my biography in every fable that I read."
— Emerson, *Journals*, 1857

"Half of all teens say they feel addicted to their mobile devices.
That's right, fifty percent of teens actually admitted they feel
addicted. Just imagine what the real number is. Not only do
teens feel they can't put their devices down, but their parents
know it (fifty-nine percent) and many parents themselves can't
put their own devices down (twenty-seven percent). This according
to a new report by Common Sense Media, which also found
that teens feel their parents are addicted as well."
— Amy Joyce, *The Washington Post*

"Technology can be our best friend, and technology can be the biggest party pooper of our lives. It interrupts our own story, interrupts our ability to have a thought or a daydream, to imagine something wonderful, because we're too busy bridging the walk from the cafeteria back to the office on the cell phone."
— Steven Spielberg

"The one thing that you have that nobody else has is you. Your voice, your mind, your story, your vision. So write and draw and build and play and dance and live as only you can."
— Neil Gaiman

"Our inner life is what makes us human, and to me, it's even more important for the way we live now. We're constantly assaulted by all kinds of things—cell phones, televisions, ads, cars, news of war, the bad economy, shootings. It's endless. Can you imagine just continuously reacting to these things? You lose your soul."
— E. Journey, *Hello, My Love*

Introduction

Something is Missing

In the beginning, like everyone else, I was in awe of all the new personal technology. It was like being a kid watching a kite flit and soar across a cobalt blue sky. It was pretty dazzling. Still, it felt at a distance and quite removed from my own reality.

Over time, more and more technology was introduced, and it began to feel as though every month a new gadget was being offered for our consumption. What started as an amazing event soon became "a bit old hat," and the onslaught of technology went from being mystical to swarming to just plain overwhelming.

Gadgets, apps, computing, consoles, video games, GPS devices, Facebook, the Internet, cell phones, BlackBerries, pagers, email, texting, blogging, pinging, surfing, and tweeting; when it comes to personal technology, our culture is overrun, and what was once spoken of as a miracle is now frequently referred to as a disturbing trend.

In recent years, there has been a growing examination of the impact of personal technology on our lives, especially those of adolescents. This has been coupled with an increasing willingness to be openly critical of a technology without limits or supervision. We now speak of it in terms of compulsion and even addiction, and this should raise a red flag.

At present, the complaining about personal technology has become incessant. Many folks simply find the phones and gadgets annoying because they take up too much time, used during times once thought to be sacred or private, like a meal, a walk, a meeting, a class, or a church or temple service. We can now claim that personal technology does not encourage real intimacy or create genuine community.

For many of us who work with teens, the impact of personal technology has become alarming. It has always been difficult in the U.S. to speak out against progress, especially technology, but I now sense a readiness in us—parents, teachers, coaches, counselors, and clergy—to speak up about the obsessive teen use of personal technology.

As a minister, I see our young people becoming more and more detached from their souls and from the nurturance of their spiritual lives. It's as if I am witnessing adolescents becoming caricatures, a quick drawing which emphasizes major external features but reveals absolutely nothing of who they really are.

I no longer allow any personal technology to enter the room at a youth gathering. The presence of such gadgetry makes it impossible to create much depth, honesty, or spirituality. Their phones can destroy a meaningful discussion or the capacity to reflect, discern, or even pray.

No, I am not scapegoating personal technology, and yes, I am aware of all the good such technology can offer, but I am also aware of the bad it may foster. I listen daily to tales of cyber bullying, kids with shorter attention spans or poor writing skills, teens who speak casually of distorted sexual expectations and a frightening lack of boundaries, and what I experience as an alarming lack of empathy or compassion.

In the past year, I have become vividly aware of one of the least addressed issues of the adolescent fixation with personal technology. I have concluded that it is stealing the time and energy and intimacy our teens require to absorb *stories*—to listen, hear, or be engaged. The loss of these stories is the equivalent of being scammed into selling their souls.

Sadly, most youth have no idea of the importance of stories and how they reveal our hopes, dreams, ideals, priorities, and heroic capacity to overcome tragedy or enable us to create in the midst of chaos as well as cope with complexities of all kinds. They are oblivious to the incredible power of stories and storytelling to help us become truly good people who pursue and achieve genuinely good lives.

But I am leaping ahead of myself.

So, let me first share the event which brought home this revelation to me, and why I now believe our youth are not only losing their stories, but possibly their very own souls.

It was a lovely evening in early December. The sky was sugared with stars. The air was cold, but not tooth-achingly cold. I was well prepared to lead our youth group discussion, and excited about its subject matter— "How to Catch the Christmas Spirit." I arrived energized about the prospects of the night's dialogue.

Twenty plus youth ambled in over the next half-hour, and each promptly slumped into a chair on the floor. I greeted each with genuine interest. They responded by asking when the pizza would arrive. I felt a twinge of irritation. I gathered my notes and wits, and following a brief prayer, presented the night's subject matter.

It was in the midst of telling them about my belief that the Christmas spirit was not an influenza we could catch, but an attitude we must choose, that I noticed their detachment. In fact, almost every one of them was talking or texting on their phones. I was about to try once again and explain why the Christmas spirit came from the inside out, and not the other way around, when I lost my temper. I erupted.

For the next ten minutes, I threw the equivalent of an adult tantrum. I told them how tired I was of competing with technology, how they were in touch with the whole world, but out of touch with one another, and how they had become the presence of an absence. This latter comment baffled them into silence, which was when I told them, "I feel like I am leading the first ever meeting of 'Mutes Anonymous!'" There was not even a giggle—I guess my tone wasn't of the jolly kind.

"Okay. Put all the cell phones and whatever away. Now! Please share with me a favorite Christmas story."

At first the silence was deafening, but then they offered up a pathetic litany of gifts they had been given on recent Christmases.

I said, "I'm not really interested in gifts. I'm asking about stories. What is your favorite Christmas story?"

The silence returned with the addition of loud squirming.

A boy named Kyle asked, "What do you mean? Like what happened last Christmas or something?"

"No. A story, a favorite family tale about catching the Christmas spirit, a special moment, a time that felt magical or even miraculous."

For the first time, I understood exactly what Stephen Hawking meant by a black hole.

Kyle, in an effort to appease his pastor, told a story about a Christmas Eve when his mom's family had made snow angels in six inches of fresh snow. It was a good effort, but it was his mother's story. I was soliciting one of their own.

"Well, now what about your stories?" I implored with interest and a forgiving spirit.

Faces again went blank, and the looks were downcast, as if ashamed.

It hit me. I was sitting with twenty plus youth who, on this subject, had nothing to say. Could it really be? They had no stories to share? I told them we would take a break and have our pizza. Maybe a memory might be jarred loose.

They immediately inhaled their pizza and went back on their cell phones, texting, tweeting, posting, or whatever. I gathered them back together and gently asked, "Don't you think it's a bit odd that you don't have a single story to share?"

I was dumbstruck. They were dumbfounded. They didn't know what the big deal was. They were puzzled by my outburst and had no idea what I was seeking from them or why the sense of urgency. I could not believe my ears or eyes or heart.

Did they really have no stories? Has the bombardment of technology replaced all the wonderful sagas of their own lives? What will happen to them if their lives become story-free? What if they have no truth telling tales to root them? What if they are never to be inspired by the words of a favorite anecdote?

I looked at them. I looked inside them. These were really good kids—a terrific bunch. I enjoyed them, and they me. There was, however, a glaring absence being revealed that night. Something was missing. If they had no stories to share, not even about Christmas, then spiritually, something was going terribly wrong.

This book was born that night. My own soul was pierced by a real fear that our youth are being raised in a culture becoming void of good stories. I was alarmed, and still am, by the possibility that technology is so strong, our culture so indifferent, that stories and storytelling are vanishing from the American landscape.

I admit it. I am a profound lover of stories, and someone who aspires to being a fine storyteller. I am also a believer that the Word of God is nothing more or less than God's own story, and we its chapters and paragraphs and sentences.

"Storytellers, by the very act of telling, communicate
a radical learning that changes lives and the world:
telling stories is a universally accessible means
through which people make meaning."
– Chris Cavanaugh

Missing Souls

As I drove home that night, I asked myself if it was just a bad night, a unique group of youth, or if I was overreacting. The answer was uniformly no. I have worked with youth for a long time, and this was an epiphany literally waiting to pounce.

I am convinced. We are seeing a new cultural phenomenon—the loss of stories and storytellers.

As I dug into the absence of stories and storytelling in our culture, I knew in my heart there must be many layers as to why this was happening. I was sure we had somehow managed to create a context conducive to the elimination of good stories.

First off, I strongly suspect many of our youth are missing their souls, or at least haven't a clue as to how to care for one. I am sure most of today's youth could not offer an adequate understanding of the concept of soul. I have asked this question at several youth gatherings, and at best they refer to the soul as the heart. This isn't a bad start, as the soul is bound to the wishes and desires of the heart, but even here their grasp is minimal.

We live in a culture which I find decidedly anti-soul. Our obsessive materialism encourages the selling of the soul. Our addiction to adolescence encourages us to stop maturing, and to be blunt, turns many of us into spoiled brats. Most of all, our youth are being taught to ignore the soul and be preoccupied with the body. Ripped abs and a ripped-out soul—not exactly a recipe for well-being, I'm afraid.

Somehow, the soul is not seen as worthy of noticing, or paying much attention to. It is dismissed as trivial, or hokey, or only for religious fanatics. Though many folks call themselves spiritual, their comprehension of the state is sadly lacking. In a culture where image is everything, the soul is simply out of step. The soul is not about image at all, but rather about claiming our humanity and genuine self.

One sure way of finding the soul is in the sharing and telling and gathering of good stories. Stories feed the soul. Stories nourish our maturation and wisdom. Stories often ignite our hopes and dreams. Stories ground and root us. Stories help create families and friendships and communities. Stories bond us together as human beings. Stories remind us of what mistakes not to make again, and to what we must aspire. Stories nourish the soul with "data" on what is genuinely good.

Kindness, courage, mercy, compassion, integrity, dignity, maturity—these are the subjects of the soul. Stories are how we address and convey this subject matter. Stories offer up a vision of the genuine good life. In today's culture, the good life ironically has little to do with goodness.

As I pulled into my driveway, I knew there had to be other missing links. The absence of stories, the neglect of the soul…both must have deep roots. This did not come out of nowhere. It must be part of a larger process, and one far more spiritually destructive than first thought.

The fact that I could not sleep was a sign to me of the urgency I was experiencing. This topic truly mattered to me. It was an ultimate concern. It was a subject my faith would demand I give my full attention. This book is the result.

"Listen to your life. See it for the fathomless mystery it is.
In the boredom and the pain of it, no less than in the
excitement and gladness: touch, taste, smell your way to the
holy and hidden heart of it, because in the last analysis all
moments are key moments, and life itself is grace."
— Frederick Buechner

Missing Childhoods

When I was eight, my father accidentally painted himself into a corner in our basement. He painted down the basement steps and into the corner by our coal bin before screaming for and at my mother to find him a way out. She yelled back that he needed to either accept doing it over, or just wait for the floor to dry. He chose the latter. He also told me to bring him coffee and three newspapers from Don Minor's pharmacy—which I promptly did.

I checked up on him over the course of the next hour, fascinated with his dilemma and determination to sit in the corner a good six or seven hours. Then an idea struck me. I would sell tickets to come and see him. I collected $2.20 at a dime a view, and my dad was surprisingly entertaining to his audience. He did a little dance. He sang some silly British ditty. He offered to be photographed. He was a great sport and taught me the gift of being able to laugh at yourself.

Many of our best stories come from our childhoods. Childhood is fertile soil for teaching us the value of stories and recognizing how stories enable us to gather wisdom. Childhood is meant to be a time of curiosity, imagination, and developing our morals and values. Childhood is intended for wonder, awe, magic, miracle, and creating unforgettable memories of all kinds.

I have come to question if many of our youth have lost their childhoods. Did they have much time to play? Were they encouraged to wander or wonder or explore? Many of our youth describe their childhood as a rigorous routine of doing—busy, busy, so busy they seldom have a chance to just be a kid.

Childhood still needs to be a time to explore and mature their senses. Many of our youth are detached from what they feel, hear, see, taste, and touch, oblivious to the body of knowledge they reveal. They also tend to have little relationship to nature. They are unaware of how their bodies and the earth itself inform them daily of what matters in life.

Many of our youth could declare their childhoods to be missing in action. By skipping this time of discovery and growth, they have been encouraged to allow technology to do the learning for them. This is a soil in which no stories can grow. It is hard baked soil. Not ready for deep roots. Not moist enough to be receptive to the seeds of true maturation or wisdom.

If a child addicted to the mesmerizing "wonders" of technology, they can leap forward in time easily and often. This is a world which has no values to impart or meaning to inspire, and could care less about a child's well-being. Service, sacrifice, satisfaction…these are the maturing themes of the stories which technology will never tell.

The bottom line is that adults are endlessly instructing children about how to make a living, but few offer much insight on how to enjoy it. It is our own stories which hold the secrets and instructions to enjoy life. We, too, have been losing track of our stories, or dismissing them as silly or inconsequential. Our kids need guidance both in locating stories and becoming storytellers. Most have had childhoods where no such guidance took place.

Missing Families

"A happy family is but an earlier heaven."
— George Bernard Shaw

The highlight of my career has been my ministry with youth. It has also been the focus of my writing. I love working with adolescents. Not adolescents who act like obedient children. Not those teens who pretend to be sophisticated adults. I enjoy those who are honestly in the midst of the turbulence of adolescence.

I am fascinated by the teen who manages to be all over the place, all of the time. Physically, emotionally, spiritually, adolescence is a period of upset and anxiety, a span of years well-known for identity crisis, the urgent search for love, and an awkward declaration of independence. It's a bumpy ride, or at least that was how it was designed.

In recent years, I have become keenly aware of the paradox which haunts so many of our youth, young parents, and families. They highly value the concept of family. They love one another, and even cherish each other—at least a few days a month. However, they are just too busy to have much time to actually be a family.

Ask a teen to name a few happy adults they know. I guarantee you will be stunned. Today's youth do not associate adulthood with happiness. They think of it as a maze of routines and responsibilities, and trying to keep everyone happy. Most youth know their parents are genuinely good people, but who don't know how to have fun. They have few good friends, are decidedly unromantic, and are worn to a frazzle.

Our youth see adulthood as an endurance test nobody passes.

Most of the youth with whom I have worked come from what I would call good homes. Yes, I have also sadly known many youth who have had to navigate the swirling currents of alcoholism, brutal divorces, and abuses of all kinds, especially the art of belittling. However, a vast majority come from homes where the heart *is* in the right place. But… the heart needs time.

The intended meaning of family and home has rapidly been dissolved by the crazy demands of our culture. It is not okay to spend a day, or even an afternoon, doing nothing. Spontaneous acts of play or re-creation are discouraged. We must check our schedules before we can come together.

Our meal times are filled with the swapping of statistics, ACT and SAT scores, grade points, class ranks, chances of getting into which college, and, of course, trying to sort through the heavy demands of getting everyone everywhere they need to go.

Family and home were meant to be a place of spiritual safety. I fit. I belong. I am accepted and understood. There is time here to talk and share our hurts, pains, dreams, and loves. This is the one place where I can be me—human, flawed, filled with worry, or bloated by joy. Home and family were meant to be our spiritual foundation, the setting for the swapping of stories from the soul. The family table was meant to be the stage upon which the dramas of our days are retold.

I am afraid this is not the case today. We are just too busy. We are too frenzied. We don't pay attention. We don't have the time to notice the inner workings of one another. Sharing intimate observations of life's lessons has been replaced with the sharing of schedules and the hellish demands on our time.

The family is not missing. The intimacy is missing. The time it takes to really know one another. The time required to create the soul of a home. The time needed to share and/or listen to a good story. Homes are like pinball machines where we bounce off one another, racking up a few points along the way, knowing full well that we are headed for the pit—going off to our respective rooms to sleep.

What I witness in my ministry is not homes filled by parents and children who dislike one another, let alone hate, but frenzied people who truly long to connect with one another. In such an environment, there is simply no room for a story to be told or heard. "We will talk about it later," has become the mantra of many American homes.

Missing Neighborhoods

When Justin was nine, I needed to make an emergency visitation at the hospital while his mother was away at a conference. I told him to stay in the house and watch his favorite movie, Watership Down, *and that I would call him every fifteen minutes until I got back home. I then told him, as a last resort, that if there was an emergency, to go to one of our neighbors. He said calmly, "But I don't know any of their names."*

I cannot even begin to tell you how sad that made me feel. I was ashamed.

Most holy books tell us to love our neighbors. Love…how can you love someone if you don't even know their name or anything about their lives? We were once a culture of front porches where neighbors gathered to share worries and wishes, regrets and hopes, tragedies and triumphs, along with coffee or lemonade or hot chocolate, depending on the season. Now we have become a nation of backyard patios with huge fences to keep the neighbors out.

Our nation often treats the neighbor with grave suspicion, as a potential enemy or opponent, or someone who will someday spread malicious gossip about us or do us dirt. I rarely hear today's young people speaking of a neighbor as a "member of the family" or as a special "aunt" or "uncle." Here again, what was once fertile ground for good stories has become a fallow field.

I remember when I was ten, my father and his three neighborhood buddies had built a huge and heavy canopy so they could watch the Friday night fights outside. Our garage was their clubhouse, and was adorned with all kinds of sports stuff and British memorabilia, including a real dart board.

On the day of the installation of what my mother called "that hideous monstrosity," and after several hours of affixing it to four home-crafted poles, the canopy was launched up into the air. My dad was yelling directions to his three pals as they sought to insert the poles into a wood base my mother said took more time to build than the pyramids.

Just then, a strong wind blew in off the lake. The four men were now moving in a zigzag pattern all over the yard. Their language was foul, and my mother and the wives of the three buddies were all shouting at the men to watch their tongues. The wind grew fierce. A driving rain fell. The men continued to weave all about the yard, cussing and groaning as they went.

The women gathered inside the garage and were laughing hysterically. I mean belly laughing. I mean hold your sides and howl laughing. They also were yelling, "I'm going to pee my pants!" which was new for us young boys to hear from the ladies of the front porch.

The canopy collapsed. The women collapsed in laughter. Even the four buddies started to laugh. I knew then that this story of the canopy collapse would become standard story fare at many summer barbecues to come.

I also knew how secure it felt to be spiritually embraced by my good neighbors and that very safe neighborhood. I knew all of their names. In a crisis, I could have gone to any home on our block and been welcomed inside and cared for.

"The Bible tells us to love our neighbors, and also to love our enemies,
probably because they are generally the same people."
– G.K. Chesterton

Missing Time

"The present is the point at which time touches eternity."
— C.S. Lewis, *Screwtape Letters*

Our culture has a horrific relationship with time. We think we can make and spend time. We sadly waste it and kill it. We foolishly talk of buying it. We brag about how we use it and how much doing we can cram into its hours. We speak of time as if it were an opponent we are required to defeat or control. We are obsessed by calendars and clocks.

We need time. We need to take time at time's word, and those words are slow and steady and simple and serene. The point of our lives is not speed. The fast lane never takes us anywhere of real value. As Lily Tomlin wisely pointed out, "The trouble with the rat race is that even if you win, you're still a rat." If we treat time as the enemy, we are always the loser.

Stories take time. They need time to be spun. They need time to be witnessed and savored. They require time to be told and heard. They need us to pay attention and notice. We cannot be held in rapture by words rattled off like a grocery list. We can't enjoy tales of truth while swallowing whole the falsehood of our busyness being of great value.

Storytelling requires stillness. A good story demands that the soul stop, ceasing from all effort to prove or do anything. A story becomes magic when it competes with nothing at all, other than for the attention of the heart, which it is ironically most capable of winning. When time stands still, the soul can begin to create the blessings of a story.

Our youth seem terrified of stopping, of being silent and still, or listening with their whole being. They seem unwilling to be settled long enough to absorb anything of real value. They are drawn to surface lives, trivial pursuits, and climbing a ladder of success—which goes nowhere at all. Our kids have abandoned stories and storytelling as an art, in large part because they rush through their days and bloat their lives with the stress of speed.

Without stories, or the time needed to tell and enjoy them, our lives become museum walls adorned by coloring book pages. These pages are neither unique nor special. This is art–of a kind—which will never move us to tears or take our breath away. Coloring book pages fail to lift our spirits, move us to higher ground, or make us better people. Coloring book pages are solely a means of teaching us how to stay within the lines. Spirituality is about the deep longing to step outside those lines.

I consider Garrison Keillor to be our greatest storyteller. He writes and delivers wondrous tales of life in a small fictional Minnesota town called Lake Wobegon. I have listened to his stories over and over again.

I can inhabit these stories. I can become a resident of this fictional Minnesotan village. Every time I listen to these small-town tales, I lose track of time. Losing track of time is like entering heaven, as heaven is the complete absence of time. A good story offers us the gracious gift of a glimpse of heaven on earth. A great story stops the clock and frees us of the oppressive notion of being on time—bound to a calendar.

Missing Lives

John Lennon once said, "Life is what happens while we are making other plans." It is a single line which caught the attention of a whole generation of young people. Its truth seared its way into our being. It carved its truth deep inside our souls. We knew he was right. We were the young who were so frenzied with planning we failed to even notice our days. We also failed to take our own stories seriously or believe they were worthy of sharing.

Our stories do matter. They need to be told. They need to be heard. They are sacred. They are holy. They are the Word of God, just as much as the words found in Holy Scripture. Our lives are written by the hand of a gracious God. A God who believes we are enough. We are his beloved children. We are cherished and adored, and we have a lot to say with our lives. In fact, our lives are "called" to express the ways we have come to know the Grace of God.

Our youth need to hear this from adults. They need to understand that the goal of making a name for oneself is far surpassed by the need to share the depth and meaning of who we really are. Who we are is found and told in our stories. Our stories define us, and bring us to life. Our stories declare our convictions, faith, hopes, dreams, and of course, the wonder of our humanity.

Our youth must come to know that their lives matter a great deal. Life matters. All of life is grace—every bit. Our youth must bear witness to the goodness and complexity and difficulty of life. They must learn to claim their fair share of the light and gain comfort within the dark.

Our youth must know they matter because of the love and mercy they can create. Love and mercy are best revealed in stories. Love and mercy express the gospel truth. Our youth must know they have been commissioned to spin a sacred yarn with their lives. Then, and only then, will they be able to behold their lives and claim they are good. Then they will be wise enough to choose not to miss out on life. Then they will know how to live a genuinely full life.

Story Starters

- What is your favorite holiday story?
- Who is the best storyteller in your family and why?
- What story best captures the soul of your childhood?
- Share an embarrassing moment which taught you to laugh at yourself.
- Tell a good story from the past week...month...year.

Section One

INTRODUCTION

A Good Story is Calling

"There is no greater agony than bearing an untold story inside you."
— Maya Angelou

"After nourishment, shelter and companionship,
stories are the thing we need most in the world."
— Philip Pullman

"We're all stories, in the end."
— Steven Moffat

Our youth are unaware they are missing stories and storytellers. I suspect they have no idea what such an absence might mean in their lives, especially to the care and nurturance of their soul. I doubt most of them have a clue why stories and storytelling are so critical to the development of a spiritual life.

I would contend that we adults have been poor caretakers of stories, and few of us have become good storytellers. We have failed to make it a priority and placed it on the back burner. We have paid far greater attention to the whims of Madison Avenue and Wall Street than we have to the stories which emanate out of our hearts, minds, souls, families, friendships, neighborhoods, and communities.

We have turned a deaf ear to the sacred sounds of good stories. A good story can enchant us and transport us to a whole different time and place. A good story often inspires courage and creativity. A good story has the divine capacity to reveal a truth and spawn values and ethics. These stories are told from the perspective of heaven, and enable us to lead truly good lives here on earth.

As adults, whether we be parents or mentors, have a responsibility to guide our youth in the discipline of story gathering and telling. We owe our young people a chance to comprehend why stories create hope in our lives and give our faith meaning. We must tell our youth why they must pay attention to a good story. We must point out the places and people where they can be heard and the communities best known for creating them.

Most of all, we must *tell* stories. We must share the stories of our lives— stories which are deeply spiritual and may move us to tears, make us die laughing, or leave us dumbstruck. We must explain to our youth how we have learned faith lessons from our lives. How we have come to understand love and forgiveness, compassion and concern, service and sacrifice. How we are nurtured in wisdom, and called to be our very best selves.

I did an exercise with the same youth group I wrote about earlier which I found to be helpful in pointing out not only the importance of stories and storytelling, but in offering them hints as to where to look and how to find such magical tales. Let me share it with you.

First, I read three obituaries to the group. Each was loaded with dates and places and people these youth did not know. Each was a composite of decades, offered up only with statistics and a few somewhat meaningful comments. I then asked them which of the three was their personal favorite, and the one individual they would have most enjoyed befriending had they been given the chance.

This group, now becoming famous for silence, began to fidget and fuss. They made a choice with as much enthusiasm as being asked to swallow sour milk. Choices were made, but only to get the task over and done with. A few did speak up and admitted they could tell nothing of substance from the obituaries or anything which actually revealed any kind of insight or intimacy. They found no clues in the lists of times, dates, places, and people. These three folks remained for them the spiritual equivalent of a cardboard cutout figures.

I then told them three stories, each garnered from having met with the family of the deceased, and each actually told at the deceased's memorial service.

The first was of a lovely lady of seventy who was a ceramic artist, a cartoonist, a fanatic fan of Melissa Etheridge, and a highly regarded harmonica player. She also traveled the world every chance she got, and she once raced on a camel and won. She ran with the bulls in Spain as a young gal and surfed until she was fifty.

Then there was a ninety-six-year-old physicist who was not only famous for his insights about the use of prisms, but whose poetry had been published in England. I read them three of his poems. One on the mystery of love, one on the wonders of sex, and one on the joy of reaching the age of ninety. (Guess which one they liked the best? Right!)

And last, a forty-seven-year-old hair dresser who went to nursing homes every wee, and did hundreds of hairdos for a buck each. She had hiked the Appalachian Trail with her husband and biked from Astoria, Oregon to New York City with her twin daughters. She was planning a bear hunt in Alaska the year before she died of breast cancer.

It was amazing how quickly each youth had locked in on the person they would be most excited to get to know. They also gave good reasons for their choices. The stories I had told, obviously of far greater length and depth than shared here, clarified their decision. The stories had helped bring these three individuals to life, or at least enough to make one more appealing than the other.

This is what stories can do. They can bring us back to life. They can bring people and places and experiences to life. They can make an idea come alive, or put meat on the bones of a dream. Stories flesh out the truth. Where the obituary told the facts of these lives, it was the stories which spoke of their personalities and their passions. Obituaries tell us what they did. Stories tell us who they were.

There are stories out there, everywhere, in everyone, calling our names, and begging to be heard. These are stories which can reach inside us and bring out our best. These are stories that long for us to know their moral or meaning, and which only desire to share with us a moment of truth.

This section is about teaching ourselves and our youth to listen up. To notice, to pay close attention, to hear about how stories are shaping us even while we sleep. If our youth are to gain the wisdom of stories and become good storytellers themselves, they will need to listen closely to how and why stories are told in the first place.

If we and our young are to listen to our lives, it will be to stories we must turn. Stories will offer us the lessons taught by how we spend and receive our days. From dawn to dusk and beyond, life is weaving a tale of truth from and for us, informing us about what matters and what will be eternal.

Stories often call us to leave the crazy world behind, reminding us how vital it often is to get a respite from the din of the world. A world of such volume, we cannot possibly hear the words of our soul, or the Word of God. The truth is that much of what is offered by personal technology is nothing more than noise, noise so loud and incessant it makes us deaf to sacred stories.

Stories call us back home. Back home to our families and friends and neighborhoods, the contexts where true intimacy and community are found, and where faith must be lived on a daily basis. Back home to our hearts and minds, feelings and thoughts, and genuine spiritual selves. Home is the seat of the soul, and the place where God can usually find us.

Stories are calling upon us to find our own callings. To figure out what it is God wishes us to do and be, and then challenging us to follow. Stories are often focused on the remarkable energy found in a life which is true to itself. Where talents are used, gifts shared, dreams disciplined, and our goals congruent with those of God.

A good story is calling. Yesterday, today, and tomorrow, a story is being woven from the faith fabric of our lives. Did you hear it? Did it sweep you away? Did it take your breath away, let you die a bit, only to be reborn a stronger and smarter soul? Did you listen with your whole being? Did you do less so that you might be able to be more?

Stories inspire and ignite. They connect us to one another. They are the ties that bind. They are the embrace of shared humanity. They are the expressions of true friendship and family and community. They are the weaving of lived prayers. They are the telling of the truth of our uniquely carved spiritual selves. They are being in touch with God, as we understand God.

This is a section devoted to the art of good listening. It is dedicated to paying attention and noticing the stories of our lives. It has a singular and most simple focus, receiving the messages being sent to us by our souls, our earth, our days and lives, those we love and adore, and a God who remains mostly mystery.

It is also a section which challenges us to choose to be quiet and still, and to remove ourselves on a regular basis from the noise and din of our scary world. We need to listen to the snowfall, and be blanketed by the wise grace of its myriad of flakes.

"It's important that we share our experiences with other people.
Your story will heal you and your story will heal somebody else.
When you tell your story you free yourself and give other people
permission to acknowledge their own story."
— Iyanla Vansant

Story Starters

- What story about you do you hope will be shared at your own funeral?
- Write your own obituary. How would you like to change the ending?
- How do stories call upon us to mature?
- How can you work on becoming a better listener and paying better attention?
- Describe the "noise" of personal technology and how it impacts you?

CHAPTER ONE

A Good Story Calls Us to Leave the Crazy World Behind

"There's always room for a story that can
transport people to another place."
— J.K. Rowling

"The stories we tell literally make the world.
If you want to change the world, you need to change your story."
— Michael Margolis

"In the time of 'information overload,' people do not need
more information. They want a story they can relate to.
— Maarten Schafer

Life is never easy. In fact, a lot of the time we have to slog our way through. If we are honest, we each have our fair share of trouble with which to contend. I am not saying we are down, depressed, or in despair. I am saying that life is difficult and demands great patience and perseverance and courage.

Why is this so hard to admit? So many of us act as if happiness is the norm and that problems rarely touch our lives. Many adolescents come to believe this fallacy, which only makes their tough adolescence even tougher. It would be so much easier, even healthier, if we adults could claim that living is quite a bumpy journey, and aging is not for the weak of heart. At least this would be telling the truth.

We adults have to embrace another truth, and this one is about the world in which our teens are living. Like it or not, it is a crazy and frightening world they are struggling to navigate.

The pursuit of money and power and possessions has become wholesale addiction. The gap between the rich and poor is hideous and widening every day. Our youth are being asked to understand why there is a third world, and how it is that three percent of the population control well over half of the wealth. The word "crazy" means absurd, ridiculous, making no sense, and this is the state of the world our youth are often being asked to accept.

They are confronted by a climate whose immune system has broken down. The ravaging of the environment threatens every living thing with extinction. Global warming is already having a dramatic impact on weather, which in turn is transforming the whole face of the global economy. Tsunamis, earthquakes, hurricanes, tornados, frigid winters, and blistering summers are no longer the stuff of the occasional disaster movie, but are the daily realities of much of the planet.

The increase in violence is staggering for us all. It is also devastating to the hope of our young—gun and gang violence, the incessant threats of terrorism, the randomness of school shootings, the secret fear of becoming the next innocent or drive by victim. These are crazy times, and the stress spawned by such a woeful lack of good sense has yet to be measured.

Our society shows warning signs of a breakdown in values, ethics, morals, and most of all, hope. I will not seek to scare you here with statistics on adolescent addiction, suicide, stress, or violent behavior.

There is no point. We all know the picture is grim. We simply must be willing to acknowledge that our youth are up against a terrifying set of odds. Their chances for health and happiness are being threatened on all sides by a world whose craziness is causing a collapse of the human spirit—and the sorry establishment of a cynical perspective in its wake.

Our youth live like there is no tomorrow. Can we blame them?

These are times of high anxiety. The frenetic pace which blankets our lives is fueled by a digital technology which is out of control, and for which our young are the "masters" and "wizards." Could it be that the technology we have created is by and large an effort to escape the world and its complex issues? Are our youth being swamped by a technology which offers them relief from the wild fears of living with such global uncertainty?

Yes, I know the irony here. The same technology which enables our youth to have the world at their fingertips is also being utilized as a quick fix to get them away from it all. This is the proverbial Catch-22. We praise our youth for their sophisticated understanding and usage of technology while failing to note it's keeping them from spiritually maturing. Technology bombards them with data while failing to address meaning and value on any level. It is as if the more they know, the less they believe they matter.

I am steadfast in my perspective that technology is swallowing up stories. It's keeping our youth transfixed but not transformed. It's creating a youthful population which no longer communicates with any degree of intimacy, honesty, or spiritual presence. Texting is hardly a soul-stirring conversation. Our youth are becoming carcasses and automatons, void of any capacity to share on a genuine spiritual basis—especially a good story.

What happens if this continues for another generation or two? What will be the result of living in the midst of such craziness and feeling so powerless to change it? What will be the impact of such a staggering loss of stories and storytellers as a result of a technology aimed at keeping our lives a game of trivial pursuits? What can we do about it? What can we *be* about it? Where do we begin?

If we are sincere in our desire to assist our youth in finding good stories, stories which calm them, center them, and enable them to feel grounded and rooted, we must begin by naming and claiming them—these are not normal times. The world is in an agitated state. It's not easy for kids to find their way through such a maze of stress and superficiality. Cynical attitudes and perspectives are hardly an effective means of coping.

If we are genuine in our wish to guide youth into healthy lives of hope and happiness, we will need to enable them to understand the immense spiritual value of a good story. We must instruct them about the capacity of a good story to free them for a time from the craziness of the world. How a story can lift them up and out of the din and doldrums of their lives. How a story can provide enchantment, and awe them with the magic and mystery and miracle of life.

Don't sell our youth short. They know the craziness of this world. They know the ruts they are already in. They long for something different—of substance, of meaning—something that might point the way to a life of real value. Our youth are smart. Their souls lie fallow only because we have not offered them legitimate spiritual options.

A Good Story is Enchanting

"You may tell a tale that takes up residence in someone's soul, becomes their blood and self and purpose. That tale will move them and drive them, and who knows what they might do because of it because of your words. That is your role, your gift."
— Erin Morgenstern

A good story is magic. A good storyteller can cast a spell which will mesmerize an audience. A good story transports us out of our present circumstances. It offers us the opportunity to transcend and to be transformed. A good story is enchanting. It fills us with wonder and awe, and the juicy joy of mystery. It scares us holy. It is tantalizing and ripe with wisdom.

When a story is truly enchanting, it as though eternity has invaded our soul. We begin to get glances and glimpses of what Heaven might look like. We imagine a world at peace. We can conceive of a time when human beings genuinely celebrate being human. A time when a world of difference is something we create and honor. Enchanting stories are like fairy tales—they can make us believe.

Most youth can easily recall their favorite book from childhood. Ask them to tell you about it. Ask them to explain why it was so captivating and had to be read again and again and again. You'll be shocked at the excellence of their recall and their insights.

The Giving Tree, The Velveteen Rabbit, The Wizard of Oz, The Missing Piece, Jonathan Livingston Seagull, The Lion, the Witch, and the Wardrobe… the list can go on and on. Such classic stories are an excellent place to recharge the spiritual batteries. These good stories are forever ready to open up and feed the soul.

The same is true of many of the great biblical parables. The stories "The Good Samaritan," "The Prodigal Son," and "The Sower and the Seeds," are easy ways to guide our youth back into the magic of a good story. A parable is a little story which packs a big spiritual wallop. We must teach our youth not only to hunt for contemporary parables, but challenge them to write one of their own.

There are also many fine stories told on film. There are tremendous dramas being staged all year long by all kinds of theatrical groups. And, of course, there is music, some of which can haunt the soul forever. The issue is taking the time to watch and read and listen. The key is being a family which seeks good stories via all kinds of mediums. Families must make decisions which support the finding of good stories, and thus, the nurturance of the soul.

Without question, our youth need to see adults taking the time to read a good book, and making sure we choose to attend a good play or film or concert. It is truly tragic if all our kids ever see is exhausted harried adults chasing a buck, but never bothering to nourish their own souls.

Do not be afraid of discussing mature subject matter with your kids. I'm not speaking about "adults only" junk, but rather that which expects our youth to bring their whole being to the encounter. Our youth live in a world which demands they know the dark side of life on an intimate basis. It cannot be eliminated. Tragically, those youth who are kept afraid of the dark find themselves too tired to enjoy their days. Enchantment is not running away from life, it is the embracing of the eternity within it.

A good story can offer us enchantment, a time of feeling blessed and knowing bliss. Good stories can be so captivating that we feel as though we have traveled far away, had ample time to re-create and relax, and are now refueled with energy and enthusiasm and excitement. We have come back to life. We are restored. To be enchanted is find joy, be ready to seize the day, and finally prepare to enjoy our very own lives.

A Good Story Lifts Us Up to Higher Ground

"Stories make us more alive, more human,
more courageous, more loving."
— Madeleine L'Engle

Good stories move us. They move us to tears. They make us laugh until it hurts. They make us change our minds or alter our perspectives. A good story pokes, prods, and pushes us forward, inviting us to mature and become more spiritual. Good stories lift us up and often land us on higher ground. A good story is always upward bound.

A good story can best be heard when we are sitting on our bottoms—physically, emotionally, and even spiritually. At the bottom we are ready to look up. There is no place else to look. At the bottom we are ready to be on the up and up as there is no point in lying—if there ever was one. When we are ready to listen up, and things are looking up, all is ripe for storytelling.

Good stories are often told during life's toughest times. They become a means of support and empathy. They stir passions of compassion and mercy. They become a way of not feeling alone and show us there are others who understand and can relate. AA and OA and NA meetings all begin with someone sharing their story, offering a glimpse into the downward spiral of addiction and the brutal impact of hitting bottom.

The fact that these stories are being told by living, breathing human beings obviously makes them inspiring.

At the bottom is often when and where we will reach out to ask for a helping hand and recognize that trying to pull ourselves up by the bootstraps can only lead to falling flat on our faces. This is the exact spiritual function of a good story. Not a helping hand, but a helping heart. A good story is one soul reaching out to another soul, offering the vision of a way to get a grip on life.

A Good Story Calls Us to the Genuine Good Life

"The most important question anyone can ask is:
What myth am I living?"
— Carl Jung

What is up there? What lies atop this higher ground? I believe it is a genuinely good life. It is a life rich in satisfaction. A way of living that has meaning and purpose, depth, and scope, and is simply our way of creating heaven on earth. It is a lifestyle which is not stylized by the media or mass market, but by our own unique vision and voice.

It bears repeating how odd it is to realize that the good life in America today has little to do with goodness. It is goodness which must be restored to the lives of our young. Goodness must be encouraged and enabled. Goodness must become a stated goal and objective. Directions must be given. Not a map, but rather pointing out the way to seek goodness.

This is the lifeblood of stories and storytelling. Good stories point out the reality of goodness in our lives and world. A good story is full of the good news—all of life is grace. Every morsel of our existence is grounded in the rich fertile soil of grace. We are composed of grace. We were created as an original blessing. We are God's beloved children, and considered worthy of God's love. We are cherished and adored. We are loved only slightly less than we are forgiven.

A good story calls us to celebrate this grace. Good stories tell us to dwell in this grace. They invite us to become one with it. They encourage us to hold onto grace when we are in short supply.

A good story challenges us to create our view of heaven in the here and now. A good story charges us to serve others, make deep and even hurtful sacrifices, and be willing to surrender. Good stories always call upon us to surrender our foolish pride, arrogance, ignorance, laziness, compulsive lying, blaming, and cheating, and most of all, the selling of our soul.

When I was eight, my grandpa witnessed me trying to roll a water-logged softball through a triangular crack at the base of our garage. He bet me five dollars I could never accomplish my goal. The next roll went straight through. He paid me five dollars (a fortune at the time), and I scooted off to Don Minor's Drug Store to buy a bunch of baseball cards.

Without my being aware, my grandpa then watched me strut around the block, showing off, and bragging about my treasure. He must have also noticed that I was giving away packs of cards. When I got back to the corner by my house, I could see him standing on the front porch stoop. I was crestfallen. I only had two packs of cards left out of fifty. I lumbered home and then burst into tears.

I had expected a long and harsh berating. Instead, I got a hug, and through my cascading tears, noticed another full five-dollar box of fifty packs of baseball cards on the top step. I was dumbstruck, but the wisdom of God had spoken. I had encountered mercy. I had been embraced by a very good man who chose to point out the meaning of the genuine good life. We all deserve a second chance.

I will never forget that event in my life, nor will I ever stop telling the story of when and where and how it happened. It is a good, simple honest story of gracious love. All good stories point out goodness to us.

Mercy, tenderness, kindness, joy, hope, wonder, love, service, sacrifice, and surrender, these are the courses required to graduate into the genuine good life.

The good life is about living in the spirit of grace. It is seeking to live without a mean bone in our bodies. It is trying to be free of the need to judge, blame, or create a scapegoat. It is trying to be the best we can be, the very soul our God created us to be.

"We had such a good time. We had such a good conversation. They are such a good friend. They have such a good heart." We do know what the real good life is all about. We also know that acquiring more and more stuff has nothing to do with an authentically good life. More and more love, more and more forgiveness, and more and more goodness. These alone are what yield a life of which we and God can be proud.

A Good Story Calls Us to Surrender

The culture is compelling. We are bombarded every day with messages to sell our soul to the highest bidder. We are counseled to believe if we do not own this product, we will never be a "somebody." We are told we literally cannot live without it. We are admonished to sacrifice our principles in favor of popularity and power. We are driven to compete in a silly and often ruthless match of materialistic pride.

We brand ourselves as winners or losers. We seek to accumulate and accomplish and achieve. We strive after security and safety. We are compulsive in our need to have it all, do it all, and be it all. We are addicted to being busy, and are often bored as hell. All of our scrambling after the culture's version of the good life leads to one lousy life, and the sad creation of what could best be called—a spoiled brat.

Good stories are wise. They know the tricks of the culture, and the many ways we are being spiritually scammed. Good stories try hard to remind us of what we know we know. We know what is bad for us and in us. We know the curse of greed. We comprehend that security and safety is never the result of a purchase. We are well aware at the core of our being, that we must sacrifice the foolishness of our culture if we are to find true meaning in our lives.

The Parable of the Prodigal Son (Luke 15:11-32) is a great story. It is the tale of a young man who basically tells his father to drop dead and then has the gall to ask him for his inheritance early. Shockingly, his father bestows the inheritance upon him as he will not deny his child the right to make his own choices.

This cocky kid had wandered off to the bright lights of the big city. His arrogant pride made him only wish to make a name for himself. He wound up squandering the whole fortune. A famine had hit the big city, and the young man was starving. He found himself at a pig trough, which is a powerful visual symbol for hitting bottom. Scripture tells us that he cames to his senses and he heads home.

When he is down the road from his home, he sees a foggy figure running toward him. It turns out to be his father, a father who had waited patiently and faithfully for his son to return and who throws his gracious arms around his son, celebrating his homecoming with a huge festive party.

"The Prodigal Son" is the story of a young man who must surrender his notion of the good life and return to the one place he knows he can find it again. The real good life, a life of love and security and belonging, a place and a space where he knows he not only fits, but has a calling. The Prodigal Son comes home to find his soul. His decision to return to his family will enable him to have a spiritual life once again.

Surrendering occurs at the bottom—at a pig trough. It is when we come to our senses and know that we must come home to the God who adores us, just like the Prodigal Son, we will be sufficiently wise enough to leave the crazy world behind and return to the welcoming arms of grace.

Good stories often ask us to come to the wilderness. It is quiet there. Solitude and stillness are ample. We can hear our heart beat, and the yearnings of our soul speak. We can potentially hear, if we really listen, the Word of God whispering on the wind.

We must listen to and for the cries and whispers of the wilderness. We must hear the prophetic wilderness voices call us home to higher ground and be true to our calling. Good stories speak from the silence, telling tales of the triumph of the human spirit over tragedy and why we must choose a better way…a road less traveled.

Our world is noisy. Our minds can be filled with din. It is not only hard to hear ourselves think, but near impossible to detect the Word of God echoing off the days of our lives. When we slow it down, grow quiet, allow a holy hush to befall us, we hear the sounds of gracious silence telling us of God's vision for our lives.

Story Starters

- What was your favorite book from childhood? Why?
- When was the last time you were moved to tears?
- Have you ever hit a "bottom?" How did you find your way back up?
- Describe what it felt like to leave home for the first time.
- Describe what it felt like to come home again.

CHAPTER TWO

A Good Story Calls Us to Come Back Home

"Home is a place you grow up wanting to leave, and grow old
wanting to get back to."
— John Ed Pearce, *Louisville Courier Journal Magazine*

"Where we love is home—home that our feet
may leave, but not our hearts."
— Oliver Wendell Homes Sr.

"My home is here. I feel just as at home overseas, but I think my roots
are here and my language is here and my rage is here and my hope
is here. You know where your home is because you've been there
long enough. You know all the peculiarities of the people around you,
because you are one of them. And naturally, memories are the most
important. Your home is where your favorite memories are."
— Pieter-Dirk Uys

Almost every good story is deeply rooted in home. To a physical place of table and hearth and rooms we call our own. To an emotional state of feeling we belong and are understood. Home is also the soul, a spiritual reality which enables us to feel centered and grounded and at peace with life. Good stories are like homing pigeons, and seem to have the instinctual capacity to return us to where we truly belong.

In recent years I have come to believe that *home* is one of the most important words or concepts not only in our language, but in the American heart. Americans will travel hundreds of miles to purchase a homemade pie or find a homegrown vegetable. We will search far and wide for an antique which captures the soul of a bygone age. We deeply yearn for those relics which recreate a simpler and saner time.

I genuinely dislike most of today's reality TV shows. These programs seem to gather together an odd collection of unstable spoiled brats. There is no true sense of home at all. No spirit of family. No soul evident in these trite and trashy shows. If this is indeed our reality, then we have become a childish, selfish nation that has hopelessly lost its way.

The power of home is best evidenced in considering a few of the great stories. These are stories which bear the message that life is a long journey home. The spiritual odyssey of our lives is the passionate urge to find our way back home again. Our eternal hope is that somehow Heaven, or our vision of it, will be much like what was once our home—or maybe our imagining of the best of what it was.

The Wizard of Oz. This is Dorothy's tornado-driven journey to Oz, only to spend her every waking second seeking to find her way back home. Why would Dorothy choose black and white and bleak old Kansas, over the thrilling Technicolor of Oz? Well, because, as Dorothy so wisely states at the end of the story, "There's no place like home." Kansas is an easy choice for Dorothy because it is the spot where her heart is filled, home to those she loves most, including her beloved pet, Toto. It is where her heart resides.

E.T., the glorious film by Steven Spielberg, provides another tale of the vital importance of home. E.T., the gentle extraterrestrial, has been stranded in the suburbs of Los Angeles. The compassion which fuels the entire film is captured in E.T.'s plea, "E.T. go home!" In wishing to go home, E.T. is no longer an alien. He becomes as human as we can imagine—our brother.

We have already reviewed the moral magic of "The Parable of the Prodigal Son" and borne witness to its message concerning a quest for home after hitting a dramatic physical, emotional, and spiritual bottom. The Prodigal Son knew in his heart of hearts there was no other place to go. He came to his senses and headed home. He was instinctually drawn to the one place he could truly heal and find hope again.

The power of the concept is revealed by these three stories since each would be a tragedy had the protagonist never made it back home. Dorothy stuck in Oz? E.T. still stranded in L.A.? The Prodigal Son still chomping down on pig slop? Without the decision to journey back home and the passionate help of others to get them there, these stories would become wicked tales with no purpose.

I have also come to suspect that homelessness is the curse not only of our culture and a horrid number of good men, women, and children living on our nation's streets, but also on a spiritual level, an issue which haunts a good number of us. We are a nation without a spiritual rudder. We lack a deep sense of home. We no longer appear to know who we are, what we are about, or where we wish to go. America is becoming a land without a vision or a voice—other than the sad spectacle of the worship of money.

America is homesick. Our youth would have a terrible time describing the American Dream in terms other than materialistic success—which is a nightmare. There is a yearning in our nation, a deep longing, to recapture a time which was quieter, and gentler, and far more compassionate. Since we cannot go back in time, we struggle to create such a spirit in our land. A land which is far more diverse in population, where problems grow more complex on a daily basis, and a world which becomes harder and harder to understand or reform.

Ours is a nation which needs many new good stories, or a revival of those that have long created hope in and for us. We need stories which will inspire us to be good people and good neighbors, and to become folks of great decency, civility, and respect. In America today, we must find a way to celebrate the diversity of race, religion, opinion, sexual orientation, and perspective.

All good stories offer us the hope of being a place and a people grounded in the Grace of God. Though I respect science, and I'm definitely a fan, I find science fiction stories only offering a way out of this world. The good stories of which I speak lead us back into the world, and challenge us to create the Kingdom of God in the here and now.

Home Is Where We Must Be Human

"Stories are a communal currency of humanity."
— Tahir Shah

It is the will of God for humans to be human. Sadly, we spend much of our time trying to be anything but human. Our youth are obsessed with being more than just human. They wish to be somebody special, to make a name for themselves, to be extraordinary, to stand out, and to be noticed.

Good stories celebrate our common humanity. Good stories lift up the gift of being average. They extoll the virtues of being ordinary. A good story reminds us that being just human is enough, and is the very essence of good living. Ordinary can be most extraordinary.

Many Americans are addicted on some level to playing God, which is always a denial of our humanity. We strive for control, being in charge, and the pursuit of perfection. We are repulsed by the notion of failure or flaw, and we are often unwilling to forgive a mistake. We are not simply a proud people—we have become arrogant and conceited. We are incessantly boasting about America and Americans being the best and the brightest.

Our young people do not seem to know how to lose with grace, survive the painful journey of maturing, or respect an opinion which differs from their own. We will go to any length to guarantee the success of our children, even murdering the young girl who may make the cheering team instead of our daughter. The absurdity of such a culture cannot be ignored or underestimated.

Good stories celebrate ordinary events. Little victories and hard-won changes. A good story tells the tale of how we must accept being human and find ways to rejoice in the humanity of others. Good stories are never judgmental or critical of others, nor do they seek to find a scapegoat to satisfy the craving for blame. Everyone has a tale to tell, a story worthy of being heard, a sacred yarn cherished by God.

Good stories erase the shame we have come to associate with being human. They encourage us to laugh at ourselves, walk humbly with our God, and grasp the truth of our simple significance. Most good stories offer up the profound wisdom that God is never interested in great success, especially financial, but is looking for those who are significant. God is cheered only by those who know when and where and how to serve others, make sacrifices which may hurt, and respect the equality of everyone.

God does not believe in the survival of the fittest. If God did, then the story of Jesus dying on a cross makes no sense at all—the gospels become nothing more than a ridiculous farce.

God believes in the capacity and need for true community to help us fulfill our dreams. We must pull one another up. We must share one another's burdens. We are called to pick up our crosses or to join in picking up someone else's. We are meant to function as brothers and sisters and respect our interdependence. It does indeed take a village to raise a child.

"The telling and hearing of stories is a bonding ritual that breaks through illusions of separateness and activates a deep sense of our collective interdependence."
— Annette Simmons

At Home in Our Own Skin

When I was in the sixth grade, I became obsessively jealous of a classmate named Zeke. He was the best athlete in the school. He looked a bit like Elvis. He wasn't a great student, but he was a tremendous artist and math whiz. He told really dirty jokes at recess which fascinated the boys and somehow attracted the girls.

During one recess, he showed his gathering of followers a checkered flag his father had won in a drag race in nearby Union Grove. I went home that night even more crestfallen than usual, as my dad was nothing more than a typewriter repairman.

As we were having dinner, my dad received a rare phone call. I heard him say that he would be over after supper and would love to see the car. Of course, I asked, "What car?" My dad explained that local boys and buddies Tony and Paul Russo raced cars, and this year their younger brother would be in the Indianapolis 500. He was going over to fix an adding machine, and would get a chance to see their race car.

A satanic seed had been planted in my heart.

The next day at recess, when Zeke was once again regaling us with the drag race story, I blurted out that my father would be the head of the pit crew for the Russo brothers at this year's Indy 500. The lie was out and quickly ballooned to gargantuan proportions.

After a hellish night of fretting the tar and feathers of shame and guilt, I went to school to face the certain revelation of my big lie. My principal,

Mr. Gregory, called me to his office, and rather than berate me for telling one whopper of a fib, he shared a lie he had told at my age which was even grander and more absurd than mine. He then told me to go out and enjoy recess, as he would take care of all of the lie's fallout.

This is, of course, a brief retelling of a lie which took on a life of its own and grew tentacles that stretched all around the school yard, to my home, and to my buddies. It is also a story which taught me a major life lesson. Do not try to be someone else. Simply accept and enjoy being exactly who you are. I was not Zeke, but I had my own share of talents, gifts, and appealing qualities. There would someday be girls who would trail after me as well—just a much shorter line.

I have never heard a good story which encouraged anyone to be phony, artificial, or somebody else. Good stories advocate for the integrity of being true to the self God gave us. Good stories invite us to grow comfortable in our own skin, satisfied with how we look, who we are, and what talents we bring to the table. Don't get me wrong, a good story often challenges us to discipline a dream or set a rigorous goal, but the basic message of every good story is that we are enough…more than enough.

Our culture is built upon keeping our population striving after more. We must own more stuff, travel more places, be known by more folks, and be more attractive. Ours is a culture which demands a makeover for us all, almost on a daily basis. We live in a belittling culture. In fact, I would contend that such belittling has often grown so compulsive it is spiritually abusive.

In a culture predicated on an economy which badgers folks into believing they need to own what they know they do not need, there is a sad tendency to quietly accept falling short. The despair of our modern culture is rooted in dragging our heads and wishing we were someone else.

We have become a society of folks who not only believe the grass is greener on the other side, but the grass on our own side has withered and died. We are not talking shades of green here, but of being a winner or a loser, a success or a failure, a somebody or a nobody. It is a vicious game, and all of us wind up losing on some spiritual level.

The most critical aspect of being at home in one's own skin is the art of acceptance. This does not mean we stop striving to improve, or have nothing we need to change, or should ignore our own flaws. What it does mean is we must come to accept we are human and a work in progress. We must learn to embrace the Grace of God, which gives us an "A" at the beginning of every day.

We are beloved children of God. We are truly cherished and adored. We are respected and believed in. We are enough. Imagine the difference in the lives of adolescents if they were raised on a steady diet of such sentiment. Would we have such a high rate of adolescent suicide were we to be a people who celebrated a basic acceptance of life on God's terms?

Home Is Where the Heart Is

The heart is the seat of all emotions. We are emotional creatures. I consider emotions to be the language of God, a sure-fire way of getting our attention, and asking us to notice if something is wrong or wonderful. There is no such thing as a bad emotion. They are simply experiences of the true feelings of the heart. The heart is the voice of the soul. An emotional message strives only to inform us of what needs to addressed, changed, dismissed, accepted, embraced, or eliminated.

Good stories are emotional. They ride waves of many different emotions. A good story may move us to tears, make us die laughing, or send a shiver up and down our spines. Good stories are planted in a garden of emotions. A good storyteller must reveal emotions with his or her voice, gestures, eyes, and spirit. An emotionless story is one which falls flat on its face.

A good story packs an emotional wallop. It lifts up emotions as a means of revealing the truth of our status, state, or spiritual condition. Emotions are not to be controlled or eliminated, but employed as a means of growing and learning.

Imagine having a loving relationship with someone who is void of emotion. Is that even possible? No, it is not. All true intimacy is saturated with emotion. Love itself is a river composed of many flowing emotions.

A good story is awash in emotions. There is no shame in being emotional. It is part of our human makeup. The more we seek to control our emotions, the more they control us. I know, emotions are tricky, and yes, they can be overindulged or used as an excuse for a vast array of abusive behavior. Still, a genuine honest expression of a feeling is not only healthy, it is also identifying and will establish a good deal of data about who we are.

As a minister, let me close this section with something dear to my own heart—the emotional impact of preaching. A good sermon is always one which arouses an emotion or two, and a good preacher is always emotionally invested in what he or she is saying. Without emotion, it is a sermon void of soul, and a sermon which resides solely in the head, is one which has lost its opportunity to inspire. Inspiration requires an emotional connection.

> "It has become appallingly obvious that our technology has exceeded our humanity."
> – Albert Einstein

At Home on This Good Earth

Good stories bring us down to earth. Though superhero stories are quite popular with kids, as they have been for a long time, maybe forever, they seldom offer adults much which entertains or informs them. Adults want to hear stories about plain old living, how to enjoy it, improve it, and make it better. Good stories offer us images of walking humbly with God upon this good earth.

A good story also celebrates the goodness of the earth. It reveals the wisdom of the seasons, the skies, and the seas. It confronts the mystery of the stars and the weather and the universe under a microscope and through a telescope. A good story is in harmony with the rhythms of the earth, including death and dying. A good story is fully cognizant of the reality that every day we are living, we are also dying.

Good stories all point to the vital importance of protecting this precious planet. Never have I heard or read a story which encouraged the manipulation or misuse of God's splendid creation. Good stories call us to be co-creators with God and to take seriously our role as stewards. This planet is our home, and this makes it God's home as well.

Good stories are relentless in their desire to call us to come back home. Stories remind us over and over again that the good life is all about good people practicing goodness, and that such goodness is really quite ordinary. These stories tell of the gospel truth that life can be lifted out of despair by one single act of compassion or kindness. Good stories speak to us of embracing the Grace of God which asks us to surrender our conditions for loving and forgiving, and to learn to live in respect and trust and genuine community.

Good stories are never about going solo, nor do they celebrate anyone's innate superiority. Good stories never call upon us to become part of some elite which sits in judgement of others. Good stories recognize how when recalling the joys of our hometowns, it is simply the gifts of neighbors and neighborhoods which are extolled. A simple life well lived, guided by grace, willing to serve and sacrifice for others, and committed to bringing one's vision of Heaven to this good earth. Now *this* is what is meant by coming back home.

Story Starters

- Describe your home as a child and today...what are the differences?
- What aspect of being human gives you the most trouble, anguish, or anxiety?
- Are you at home in your own skin? Why or why not?
- When and where and with whom do you feel the most centered or totally lose focus?
- How has Mother Nature served as a spiritual tutor or mentor in your life? Why do we call it Mother Nature and Mother Earth?

CHAPTER THREE

A Good Story Calls Us to Our Very Best Selves

"Ideals are like the stars. We never reach them but, like the
mariners on the sea, we chart our course by them."
– Carl Schurz

"The ideals which have lighted my way, and time after time
have given me the new courage to face life cheerfully,
have been kindness, beauty and truth."
– Albert Einstein, *Ideas and Opinions*

A good story can move us, motivate us, make us better, heal our soul, mend a spiritual fence, and offer us meaning in this life of ours. Good stories are always calling. They are being acted out in the dramas of our days. They are being told before meals, around fires, over a glass of wine, and by the stranger passing us on the street. They are everywhere, and they are for everyone. These stories raise the bar. A good story can lift us up. A good story expects our very best.

Being a Good Host

"I force people to have coffee with me, just because I don't trust that a friendship can be maintained without any other senses besides a computer or cellphone screen."
— John Cusack

My late good friend, Forrest Church, beloved Unitarian pastor and prolific author, was an extraordinary host. If I were to say this to most adolescents today, they would nod, but have little understanding of the concept of hosting. We live in a time and culture which has dismissed the notion of being a good host and its spiritual importance.

I attended many gatherings at Forrest's summer home on Shelter Island. These were casual affairs, focused on a good meal and great conversation among interesting folks. The guest list and menu were chosen with whimsy and a sense of summer being a time to play. I will add here that Forrest's wife, Carolyn, was crucial in the creation of such joyous events. Carolyn took charge of the meal, and Forrest the conversation, and then during the course of the event they magically, as if on cue, swapped duties.

What made Forrest such a great host was how he made his guests feel. The art of hosting is truly a matter of attitude and perspective and the real work of intimacy. Forrest made us feel welcome, wanted, and special.

I was made to know I belonged, and Forrest somehow let it be known I had something of value to say. Forrest affirmed me and let other guests know I was important to him. It was a gift to receive, and it mattered a great deal to me—especially now in its absence.

Our youth need to know how to be good hosts. They need to acquire the wonderful skills of paying attention, taking note, being empathetic, listening well, encouraging others to share, shining the spotlight on someone other than themselves, and lifting up the presence of another soul. The art of friendship is grounded in being a good host, as is the spiritual discipline of loving our neighbor as ourselves.

I never left a gathering at Forrest and Carolyn's where I did not feel better. This is an amazing talent and one of the true callings of love. It was not that I left thinking myself to be better than others, or being of select company. It was simply to believe again in how good life could be. A good storyteller enabling good stories to be shared makes for a miracle of an evening, and sadly, this is an experience few young people have ever had.

Being Sabbath for Others

"Turn off your email; turn off your phone; disconnect from the Internet; figure out a way to set limits so you can concentrate when you need to, and disengage when you need to. Technology is a good servant but a bad master."
– Gretchen Rubin

There are two observations I have made toward the end of my ministry which not only stand out, but plead their case on a daily basis. First, I have become keenly aware of just how weary many of us are. We are so busy we can barely breathe, and the lists which dictate our lives keep getting longer and longer. Expectations scale ever new heights, while rewards and gratification swiftly diminish. We are ripe for being burned out. The fire in many of our hearths has either gone out or is barely smoldering. Thus, our youth are being raised and taught and mentored by adults whose energy supply is almost non-existent.

Second, I have noticed more and more how folks no longer observe any kind of Sabbath—in America days of rest are not allowed. This addiction to activity, belief in the demand for ever increasing speed, and the neurotic drive to do it all, is creating a physically, emotionally, and spiritually exhausted population. We are a people ripe for the picking, and what is choosing us is a wide range of stress related diseases and conditions.

Good stories are born, grow, thrive, and become alive within a context of Sabbath. When we are at rest, we can imagine, or daydream, or reflect on the holiness which is knocking on the soul's door. Our youth must learn how to slow down, stop, look and listen, and do nothing for periods of time. This is what is meant by the Sabbath.

There were days of rest, even for God.

Good stories are told during such Sabbath times. They are shared around a campfire, over a lazy meal, on a front porch, a long walk, and when the day is settling and the evening's air is ripe for gracious words. When was the last Sabbath time you experienced? When did your teen last take time to ponder, reflect, wonder, wander, or be a child-like spirit? When were they free to receive the day rather than to try and conquer it?

Most good stories are good at telling us to slow down and open ourselves to what the day has to say. Good stories offer the soul an experience of Sabbath. They give us the good gift of rest, and remind us all will be well. They tell us life is not in our clutching little hands, but under the guidance of a much higher power. They get us off the hook of trying to be in control, in charge, or needing to find all the answers.

"Soon silence will have passed into legend. Man has turned his back on silence. Day after day he invents machines and devices that increase noise and distract humanity from the essence of life, contemplation, meditation...tooting, howling, screeching, booming, crashing, whistling, grinding, and trilling bolster his ego. His inhuman void spreads monstrously like a gray vegetation."

– Jean Arp

How to Be Holy

"There are few times that I feel more at peace, more in tune,
more Zen, if you will, than when I force myself to unplug."
– Harlan Cohen, Six Years

*I recall leading an autumn retreat several years back that was called,
"Harvesting the Holiness." The first session was a disaster. I could not
understand why none of my material was catching fire. Why there appeared
to be little interest or recognition of the value of the topic.*

*At the first break of the evening, which I sought with relish, one of the
participants and a good friend said, "So you are going to teach us how to be
holy rollers this weekend?" It had never dawned on me how the word "holy"
was wrought with so many negative connotations. Holy rollers, holier than
thou, trying to be a saint, and on and on. Before any good discussion could
occur, we needed to establish a more positive understanding of the concept
of "holy."*

This is even truer today, and for our teens, the concept of holiness is
coated in self-righteousness. I believe our youth need to understand the
true meaning of holiness. They need to know how to look and listen for
it, where to hopefully find it, how to inspire it, and most of all, how to
become its follower.

Good stories often teach an important truth—holiness is not about being perfect. Even the biblical stories are filled with the sagas of holy sinners, from Moses the murderer, to Judas the betrayer, Thomas the doubter, Peter the denier, and the whole history of the flawed and often foolish Church. If God wanted perfection, God would not have chosen the Jews or the disciples as role models—what a motley cast of characters.

Good stories quietly share the divine truth that holiness is about wholeness, not perfection. The pursuit of perfection is usually demoralizing. The pursuit of excellence is quite invigorating. Holiness expects excellence of us, not perfection. Excellence is possible for humanity. Perfection is simply not. Good stories accept life's terms, and the guaranteed imperfection of humanity is atop that list.

Peter Havey was a fine fragile young boy who had recently lost his mother to a swift savage cancer. I was to conduct his mother's funeral, and for some uncanny reason, Peter knew it would be a major emotional struggle for me. His mother was a woman of exceptional goodness and grace, and someone I suspected had suffered a most sordid family history. Just before the service, Peter came up to me and gave me a hug and asked if I was okay. I told him he was intruding on my lines. We both laughed.

I wept openly during the readings and hymns, but I tried quite hard to pull it together to deliver my tribute to Susan. Through my entire eulogy I noticed Peter nodding at me, nodding a message of reassurance and appreciation, nodding to let me know whatever I said would be more than fine, nodding to let me know he and his mother approved.

Peter's nod was a holy act. I do not think Peter knew this to be the case in giving it, but I knew it in receiving it. What made it so holy was how this young boy had captured his mother's spirit at the funeral, by putting my needs way ahead of his own.

Holiness can take us beyond. Way beyond what we ever dreamed we could do or be, and far past what we may have long accepted as our limits. The holy is when our human spirit merges with the Holy Spirit, a transforming moment when we become one with God. In these holy moments life seems too good not to be true, and death imparts no fear at all.

We have all known such times of divine-human merger. It might have come while beholding nature's beauty; the embrace of a child at bedtime; the capturing of a first snowflake on the tongue; or the joy of knowing one is forgiven. Such moments can take our breath away, and we are reborn. We become brand new. Holiness erases age, and does so by banning Time from having a stranglehold on us. When we become holy, we are functioning according to the principles of eternity.

When was the last time you completely lost track of time? Whenever it was, or whatever you were doing or being, you were in a holy context. You had stepped quietly and unintentionally into heaven. You were being embraced by the absence of time, which is the spiritual essence of eternity.

Good stories share such holy moments in our lives. They serve as the wonderful host who helps us fit in, and to be confident in the telling of our own story. A good storyteller begins the telling of the tale with one true hope, and that is to capture our imagination, and lift up our souls to higher ground. A good story always seeks to make us better, and in so doing to participate in God's holy effort to transform us and keep us fresh and new.

"Stories have to be told, or they die, and when they die, we can't remember who we are and why we're here."
– Sue Monk Kidd

Story Starters

- When was the last time you felt you were functioning as your very best self?
- Who would you call a great host and why?
- Describe your perfect Sabbath day of rest.
- Explain to an adolescent, what it means to choose to create a Sabbath day and keep it holy.
- Define holiness and then ask yourself where and when and how you find it?

CHAPTER FOUR

A Good Story Calls Us to Make a Life

"The feeling of being hurried is not usually the result of
living a full life and having no time. It is, rather, born
of a vague fear that we are wasting our life."
— Eric Hoffer

"Life is uncharted territory. It reveals its story one moment at a time."
— Leo Buscaglia, *Executive Health Report*

This is one of my all-time favorite stories. It is true. It was a defining moment in my life, and especially my ministry. It is a story on how to make a wonderful life.

Judy Trentadue had been a great friend at my first pastoral call, Bay Shore Lutheran Church in Whitefish Bay, Wisconsin. Her cancer was sudden, and her demise swift. Her death came as no shock, and yet it upended my world for weeks and months.

Judy was truly beautiful. She was sweet and kind and tender-hearted. She brought joy to a room. She had a spirit which sparkled, and a heart which gave meaning to the concept "aglow." She had a great attitude, kept life in perspective, always reminding herself that the little things were most often the truly big things. She was a pretty petite woman who knew the magic of a little loving, a little laughing, a little forgiving, and a little faith. She left a legacy of grace for her cherished husband and three adored and adoring children. She is remembered to this day as a spiritual role model, for me and I suspect hundreds of others.

At the close of her funeral, which was literally mobbed and the largest I conducted at Bay Shore, I ducked out for a breath of air and a weep. I was standing on the back stoop to the church offices when a little blond boy with wide blue eyes stopped on his bike and asked me why I was wearing a dress. I told him I was a minister, and it was a tradition. (I wanted to tell him I had no idea who the sadist was who had dreamed up this crazy uniform.) He then asked me who had died, as he had noticed the hearse. I told him her name, to which he then asked, "And why was she so famous?" I told him she really wasn't, but then he turned and pointed to the packed parking lot and the cars lining the street for what must have seemed to him like miles.

I recall telling the little boy on the small bike that Judy was famous for her goodness. He told me he didn't understand. I smiled and wanted to tell him I did not fully understand, either. I did tell him that someday he would understand. At that point in my ministry, I truly did believe he would someday comprehend Judy's subtle fame. At this point, I am no longer so sure. Our children seem to have little to no grasp of how memorable goodness can be and why it must be sought in the genuinely good life.

He pedaled off, and I remember feeling moved to tears, to hope, even to faith. Judy's simple ordinary unnoteworthy life was not only worthy of fame, it was my job to instill her legacy in the lives of the youth with whom I would work. I wanted them to know Judy's secret, which was she had a made a most modest living as a hairdresser, but she had managed to make a life which was transcendent. Judy was unforgettable. That is why the parking lot was packed, and a small blue-eyed boy would ask how she got famous. She was famous for her loving and caring and goodness. In making a life, more than merely a living, she had fulfilled God's hope for her.

"Telling stories is not just a way of passing time. It is the way wisdom is passed along. The stuff that helps us live a life worth remembering."
— Rachel Naomi Remen

Making Do

"A human being's first responsibility
is to shake hands with himself."
— Henry Winkler

The foundation of many good stories is to tell folks how to make do. Making do means acceptance. It is the art of not needing to have it all, and instead working with what we have. It is the practice of doing less so that we might be more. It is the discipline of longing for less, rather than always grasping after more.

It is the measure of enough. Enough is enough. Those who make do are those who understand how much our lives need balance. Making a life is the creation of such balance and the result is our well-being.

Our youth need to learn how to make do and quit whining about what they must have. They are in dire need of maturing. Most good stories reveal the skills and secrets, and even a few tricks, in the process of growing up. Making do is high on that list. It is a mindset, an attitude, and a perspective. It is the acceptance of boundaries and borders. Maturity requires the soul to know how to say no.

In our culture of "never enough," personal technology displays our addictive nature. Our youth panic when kept from technology, and seem unable to make do for a moment without being in contact with everyone they know. Technology itself seems resistant to boundaries. Every day there are new gadgets and devices, which will in turn create the need for even more sophisticated or speedier technology. It is a vicious cycle, and it's spiritually destructive.

Make It Happen

"Well done is better than well said."
— Benjamin Franklin

All good stories have one thing prominently in common. They tell us of folks who walked the walk, and went beyond just talking the talk. They made things happen. They took action. They created and carved out a dream. They were true makers.

I recall the Hansen's, a lovely couple with five equally lovely children. At many family gatherings in their warm and cozy home, other guests would make mention of what a wonderful family they had. Bill, the beloved patriarch, would always say, "Well, we made it happen. It was one hell of a lot of work." Janet, the adored Mom, would add, "Yes we did, and yes it was—very hard work!"

I loved this honesty. I loved that they caught folks off guard by acknowledging that good kids and a good family don't just drop out of the air and into our laps. It does require a great deal of patience and perseverance, and the determination to make it happen. I am not saying it will work every time. I have known many a family which imploded or exploded for reasons which had little or nothing to do with anything or anyone but unpredictable life itself. However, in a vast majority of cases, the creation of a good family was one ton of hard work.

Our youth need to grasp the importance of the word, "making." It is a simple concept, and yet it embodies the full idea of getting down to the work. It is about movement and action and getting something done. When we sit down to a great meal, we are being rewarded by the effort of the meal maker. A great deal of planning, time, effort, and talent went into its delivery. It isn't magic. It is focused energy and love.

I remember my late wife, Christine's, church had T-shirts made which read, "Peace in Search of Makers." They were popular. Everyone understood the message. So many people spouting off about peace, but so few making it happen.

"Making." The image of being not only busy, but productive, and creating something which is good. Making a living is all about getting busy doing, and being good, and actualizing our dreams. Good stories tell us of folks who have made their wishes and hopes come true.

"Life is a great big canvas,
and you should throw all the paint on it you can."
— Danny Kaye

Making a Difference

"No matter what you do in your life, what you create,
what career you have...your greatest creation is
always going to be your life's story."
— Jonathan Harris

Good stories tell us of people who have made a difference. Not always a big difference and not always having achieved a big name for themselves. Good stories often tell us of the impact of the little things in life. They speak to us of how a little patience can prevent someone from making a horrible choice, or how a little perseverance might enable an individual to accomplish a life-long goal, or how a little forgiveness can heal a marriage or friendship or family. Good stories focus on the many small ways we can make life better.

I remember getting off the airplane from Minneapolis, coming home for my fall break from St. Olaf College. I had been a nervous wreck all day and had a horrid headache from the bumpy flight, only to see my father waiting for me and openly weeping. I was shocked. I had never recognized how much I mattered to him, nor was I aware of just how much he mattered to me. We had made a huge difference to one another and had done so in so many small ways.

A good storyteller takes a story the size of a seed and plants it in the human soul. It is often a seed of someone making a difference in someone else's life. It is often a simple tale of how a smile, a compliment or criticism, a gift, a word of encouragement or advice, or a gesture of love or forgiveness, had served as a turning point. How a difference can be made by the tiniest gesture or simplest word.

We need to inform our youth about how important it is to spend their days wisely. How making a life is all about making a difference. At the end of the day or a life, nobody will recall the size of one's bank account or the price of their car, but they will be remembered for the quality of their loving and their mercy.

Have you made a difference today? This should be a question we ask of ourselves and our youth. It is an inquiry we need to conduct at the dinner table or at a holiday gathering. Our young people need to know how others have touched a life and how they might do so as well.

Making It Count

"We need to look hard at the stories we create and wrestle with them. Retell and retell them, and work with them like clay. It is in the retelling and the returning that they give us their wisdom."
– Marni Gillard

Our youth are being raised in a disposable culture. Their computers and other technological gadgets are quickly out of date. They have been taught to be slaves to what is in fashion. They have learned to accept the rules of an economy built on obsolescence. Our culture is also derelict in paying attention to the lessons of the past while failing to develop a true vision for a livable future.

It is a good thing to live in the moment. It is a very bad thing to live in a moment you fail to pay any attention to. Then life becomes nothing but a blur of busyness.

Making a life requires that we be willing to wait. It tells us that slow is often better, and that there is great meaning in having persevered and accomplished a difficult task. Making a life is to make our lives matter. It is to take life seriously, and ourselves less so. It is making choices and knowing the consequences. It is about making decisions which are compassionate toward others, the earth, and life as a whole.

Good stories lift up the lives of those who accept the high cost of the real good life. The discipline, the determination, the drive needed to build a bit of heaven on this good earth. Good stories speak to us of those who understand that eternity is how long true goodness will last, and that pleasing God is all about creating eternity in our midst.

"Information overload is a symptom of our desire to
not focus on what's important. It is a choice."
— Brian Solis

Making a Miracle

"This is the sorcery of literature. We are healed by our stories."
— Terre Tempest Williams

Miracles last. They are never fully explained, and always remain at heart a mystery. They are experienced by everyone, and claimed by few. The fear of being thought "nuts" remains a powerful threat. Still, good stories over the years have revealed a steady stream of events which make no sense, defy the odds, prove to be unexplainable, and yet remain obvious and true, at least from the perspective of those who experienced them.

I have come to believe that when miracles are linked to making money, my eyebrows raise, my attitude sours, and I become a skeptic. Miracles of the gospel truth variety seem to always be free of money making. The good stories about miracles never have an ending about how the miracle made a bundle of bucks. The true miracles remain simple, unexpected, stunning, transforming, upending, and difficult to capture in words—never defined.

I have also concluded that we all have miracle stories tucked away in our hearts, minds, and souls. We all have memories of events or experiences which left us speechless, or sent a shiver up and down our spine, or made us feel as though God were truly present, even if we could not find the words. When given a chance to share them, and the time needed to dig them up, I am stunned by the beauty and clarity of so many of these simple tales.

Ruth was my secretary on Shelter Island for ten years. She was a brilliant and kind woman, with enormous integrity and a fearless faith. When she called, her voice told me I needed to come right away. Ruth never asked for much, and an invitation for coffee and conversation was rare for her.

I arrived on a rainy day, and Ruth met me with a steaming hot cup of coffee. We went to the living room in her lovely home and sat before a glorious fire. She told me how earlier that afternoon, she had cozied herself under an afghan, was reading a good new book, and enjoying a glass of wine by the fire, when suddenly, and most unexpectedly, the fire went out. Ruth next told me that at that very moment she sat up and knew her mother was dead. The link between these events might appear clear only to Ruth, but she had not a single question as to their eternal bond.

Just before she called me, Ruth received a call from a sibling to tell her of the bad news she already knew. She managed to pretend she did not know, and shared a deep appreciation for the call. She was assured funeral details would be made later, and again stressed how glad she was to know. In calling me, Ruth had decided she could not hold the miracle in any longer. Like most miracles, this one would manage to find a way out into the fresh air of faith.

As I sat with Ruth, I realized something about her. Ruth was a woman of strength, wisdom, and courage. She was also a worthy recipient of a miracle. By worthy I mean ready to receive one. Ruth was insightful, sensitive, empathetic, compassionate, and quietly passionate. I believed then, as I do now, that God knows with whom miracles can be shared. Could it be that his selection of disciples was made from being aware as to who was most likely to see and hear and touch him after he had passed—another mystery?

Like Ruth, I suspect we can create an environment in which miracles are likely to occur. We may not create the miracle itself, but we can indeed set the stage, till the soil, and prepare the soul for its reception. We can do so by being spiritually aware, wide open and awake, sensitive of heart, keen of mind, willing to mature at a moment's notice, and paying attention to and for the presence of God in our lives.

Making a miracle is about taking note, having the pen and paper in hand, ready to claim a miraculous event or experience. I wonder sometimes how many miracles a day we forget, or simply fail to even notice.

Life is a miracle. Good stories herald this truth. All of life is miraculous, from its inception to its ending and *beyond*—as well as the oft forgotten, *before*. A good story becomes good in the listening, and when a soul is ready to receive its message and meaning. Good stories point at the many miracles which dot our lives, asking us to connect those dots over time, and thus ultimately see the face of God.

> "There is no greater power on this earth than story."
> – Libba Bray

Making a living bears little resemblance to making a life. One is focused solely on the self, while the other is laser focused on locating God. One is all about accumulation and the other is about knowing we actually own nothing. One is all about thinking ourselves to be something really special, and the other finds the miracle in ordinary living. One is all about achievement, and the other is about the wisdom of receiving.

It is hard to write a good story about making a living, as it is too predictable, and holds no more fascination than a paint-by-number landscape. Only making a life holds our interest and our breath, and makes us yearn to know the end of the story, assured that it will have a good ending, as all truly good stories must. A good story, especially one about making a life, will possess an ending which will be transformed by goodness in the telling.

"...the secret of the Great Stories is that they have no secrets. The Great Stories are the ones you have heard and want to hear again. The ones you can enter anywhere and inhabit comfortably. They don't deceive you with thrills and trick endings. They don't surprise you with the unforeseen. They are as familiar as the house you live in. Or the smell of your lover's skin. You know how they end, yet you listen as though you don't. In the way that although you know you will one day die, you live as though you won't. In the great Great Stories, you know who lives, who dies, who finds love, who doesn't. And yet you want to know again. That is their mystery and their magic."
– Arundhati Roy, *The God of Small Things*

Story Starters

- Share a recent time you consciously choose to create an act of goodness.
- Who is the most merciful person you know?
- Who has made the biggest spiritual difference in your life?
- How have you made a noteworthy difference in someone's spiritual life?
- Define a miracle. Can you share a family story which can be described as one?

CHAPTER FIVE

A Good Story Calls Us to Create a Calling

"No one is useless in the world who lightens
the burden of it for anyone else."
– Charles Dickens

"I have always held firmly to the thought that each one of us
can do a little to bring some portion of misery to an end."
– Albert Schweitzer

It was early autumn. I had been leading a retreat in Lake Geneva and decided I needed a retreat from the retreat. I went down to the lake at sunset and went out to the end of the pier at Covenant Harbor. The fiery trees were reflected in the lake like a Monet painting. It was so lovely and haunting it took my breath away. It was what I needed. A little "mini-death," so I could revive my weary soul. I fell sound asleep.

I woke up around two, maybe three hours later. A wind had blown in, and the temperature had dropped a full twenty degrees. It was pitch black, and I suspected all the retreat participants had headed into town for dinner. We were not due to gather back up until 10:00 p.m. for a closing devotional. I stood to walk back in and quickly realized I couldn't see the shore or even the pier, nor was I able to walk on something which was no longer floating, but bumping and grinding atop the choppy water. I quickly sat back down.

I felt anxious. I knew this was stupid. I doubted the water was all that deep. The retreat folks would certainly be returning in short order. But what if the wind picked up even more or it started to rain? The idea of waiting another hour or more seemed daunting. Plus, I would feel and look so stupid, and it was also pretty damn cold. I felt chilled, and noticed I was beginning to be sprayed by the water. Great. My teeth would be chattering soon.

About thirty minutes later, I heard a man's soft voice. He reminded me of the sweet-sounding Red Skelton my father never missed on TV in the '50s. Skelton always offered a blessing at the end of his show, and he sounded like a Grandpa tucking in a favorite grandchild. This was that kind of voice. I suddenly recognized it was Dan, a man from Waukesha I had met at that day's lunch.

"Reverend Grimbol, is that you out there?"

"Yep, that would be me. I'm glad you can see me because I cannot make you out at all."

"The water sort of frames you out there."

"Thank God."

"Is there a reason you're not coming in? We came back to see if you wanted to join us for some pizza and beer."

The very thought was worthy of singing the doxology.

"I truly cannot see the shore, and the pier is doing one nasty bump and grind."

"Oh. I see." We laughed heartily. "I tell you what, why don't you crawl, and I will guide you in by voice."

"Deal!"

And so I skinned my knees on a journey back to shore as I followed the voice of Dan chanting my name. We had a good hug and laugh upon my arrival on the sand. I must admit to a relief which was far more considerable than the dimensions of the crisis.

I think God is always playing Dan's role, even the part about asking us to get on our knees. Maybe not all of the time, but there are definitely times we need to be in that very dependent position. God is calling us to solid ground. God is bringing us back to higher ground. God is offering us the guidance needed to find our way back home. God is chanting our name into the silence. God's voice is leading us to the safety of the shore.

It is my conviction that one of the primary ways God speaks to us is with stories. These stories often provide us with a message which will map a way of return to life and to God—as well as our genuine selves. Stories which point to a simpler way and beckon us to be wise enough to follow. If we are listening, which is not often these days, and open to hearing, God is calling us to new adventures every single day. God's call is one which wants an abundant life for us. A life filled with meaning and purpose and value. God is calling us home to the heart and soul.

I was smart enough to follow Dan's voice. My slow wobbly crawl was neither pleasant nor graceful, but it was an easy decision to make, as there was no place else to go, and no other way to get there—except for a chilly choppy swim I did not wish to make.

Are we smart enough to follow God's call when we hear it? Will we take the risk and accept the embarrassment and make our way back to a genuinely good life? Will we pay attention to a God who is ceaselessly seeking us out? Will we take note of the many ways God is trying to reach us, especially in the stories of our lives?

Good stories help us immeasurably in creating a calling. They speak to us of what matters and that which is eternal. They tell us the gospel truth and remind us of what we know to be true. They lift up before us the urgency of our compassion and care and concern, the yearning of our kindness and graciousness and generosity, and our capacity to make a difference by choosing to serve and sacrifice and be the people we were created to be.

Trust me on this. Creating a calling is not easy in our modern world. The din of our busyness and our culture's obsession with accumulation and success make it hard to hear the sweet and simple stories of another way. For our youth, it's near impossible.

We have to fight for their attention. We need to insist on teaching them the immense importance of listening. In many cases, we will be forced to introduce them to nature, their souls, prayer, worship, meditation, and the joys of genuine communion and community.

We have our work cut out for us. A calling is the work of a lifetime. It is the expression of God's devotion and adoration for us. It is a clear statement that we are indeed God's beloved children. Like all art, it may look easy, but it requires focus, discipline, energy, and a steadfast faith in why it is worth the effort.

"Each of us is a book waiting to be written and that book,
if written, results in a person explained."
– Thomas M. Cirignano

Called to Stop

"...a wealth of information creates a poverty of attention..."
— Herbert A. Simon

There is one great truth in the art of telling a good story. It requires that everything stop around it. The story must be the sole focus, and the audience must grow still, silent, and willing to go on a journey of the soul.

Without everything stopping, as if holding its collective breath, the story will not have a chance to be truly heard. The power of a story rests upon a foundation of spirit speaking to spirit, which is the all-encompassing busyness of doing nothing in order to become everything. For a story to do its work and to be in action, it demands that the listener be willing to surrender all other activity in order that they can be still and know God.

The spiritual discipline of stopping is crucial to creativity. Like the baby who slows and rests before birth, the soul must wind down and prepare to be transformed. We must become a culture at ease with the notion of stopping—doing not one blooming thing, being as still as an egret in the water with eyes on an insect or fish.

Most of us have restless mind syndrome. We are chronic worriers and list makers, and we keep track of when, where, and how to do it all. This is the call to burn-out. It is a recipe for exhaustion. It is a disaster in the making. To find our truest calling, we must turn off our minds and enter our hearts. We must be in touch with our souls and listen to and for the Word of God – especially that which is shared in stories.

The spiritual life begins with *stop*. We must stop trying to be in control. Stop trying to be in charge. Stop trying to keep everyone happy. Stop trying to be perfect. Stop seeking to play God. Stop...it is the first step of spiritual surrender.

Our youth will have a terrible time with the idea of stopping. Other than being in bed with covers over their heads, adolescents find stopping almost physically impossible and emotionally and spiritually frightening as hell. I cannot tell you how vital it is for us to teach our kids to know when and where and how to *stop*.

It is so crucial that our youth recognize how true maturity is rooted in creating a balanced life. A huge part of that balance is located not only in the wisdom of rest, but also in simply stopping everything. We owe our kids a chance to know themselves and their God. We need to get off their backs about being endlessly busy, driven, neurotic, and young workaholics. This is not healthy, nor does it nourish the soul.

There is simply not a workaholic anywhere who has time to listen to a good story. In fact, the one they listen to least is the one being written by their own being. They are often deaf to their own calling.

"If you can spend a perfectly useless afternoon in a perfectly useless manner, you have learned how to live."
– Lin Yutang

Called to Small

"A little kindness from person to person is better
than a vast love for all humankind."
– Richard Dhemel

Stories are small. There may be a wide-scoped epic, or a sweeping saga told now and then, but most stories are simple, straightforward tales which can be told in minutes, not hours. As we gather at a holiday table and feast, the dessert and coffee are often accompanied with such tales. Sweet and stirring anecdotes and parables which reveal a moral or ethical lesson, or the inspiring words of a gifted storyteller determined to make us laugh or cry or both.

These little stories often witness to the extraordinary importance of making a little difference. In a culture which celebrates the big and the bold, these stories do the opposite. They call attention to simple acts of kindness, decency, compassion, concern, self-sacrifice, and unconditional loving and forgiving.

These brief stories grasp the grace made available in a moment— when someone chooses to be the best they can be and makes a difference in someone's life. Many of these lovely little stories tell of how someone made someone else's day, and by doing so, wound up creating a major shift in the path of a whole life. These tiny tales are the seeds of heaven being planted here on earth.

I believe that God calls us in such small stories. God also calls us to lead small lives. A small life is not a life in miniature, but one focused on what truly matters and honors that which has eternal value and worth. God is not looking for us to change the world, but rather to change a heart or mind or soul.

God is not asking us to perform miracles, but to bear witness to those daily happenings which give us a lump in the throat, a shiver up and down the spine, or a goose bump or two. God is not asking us to build another Tower of Babel, but to be wise enough to know we don't need to climb up to God, for God will daily reach down to us.

Our youth need to come to understand small as a way of life. Small is what is meant by humility. Small is what is called for in sharing. Small is how we make a difference and build the Kingdom of God. Our lives are not about the big splash, or the notoriety, or how we have managed to impress the culture. A celebrity is usually known solely for being known.

It is the genuine good life which impresses God, and these small stories tell of those good folks whose goodness is shown in a myriad of ways and on a daily basis. In a world of such selfishness and greed, and such a glut of excess, how wonderful it is, even relieving, to hear the stories of the power of small.

The last year of my wife Patty's life was brutal. She was in incessant and awful pain, and her dignity had been torn to shreds. It was hard to imagine how she managed to find the will to get through a day, but she did. My son, Justin, would often arrive in the afternoons with two cold beers, a chocolate bar, and a true tearjerker of a movie. They would sit under an afghan and enjoy having a beer, a chocolate, and a good cry.

Such a simple thing, but it made such a huge difference in Patty's last days. I was deeply touched by the kindness, wisdom, maturity, and raw goodness of my son. I share this little story with as many as will listen. It is the stuff of the fifth Gospel—what we write with our little stories, our little lives, and a small mustard seed of faith.

"None are so empty as those who are full of themselves."
— Benjamin Whichcote

Called to Serve

"We are becoming the servants in thought, as in action,
of the machine we have created to serve us."
— John Kenneth Galbraith

Ask a group of youth to tell you about the last time they served someone. Serve—as in putting another's wants and needs ahead of your own or to make another individual the sole focus of your attention. Most young people will have a story to tell, which is indeed a good thing, but there will likely be a few oddities you will quickly notice.

These acts of service are usually spoken of as a special event, a project, or an activity coordinated by a group. Serving someone will be recalled not as a frequent or daily endeavor, but as a carefully coordinated happening. Though pride may be claimed, the stories shared reveal how genuine acts of service are not par for the course, but rather a rare exception.

Our young people are simply not expected to serve. Our culture's distaste for the role of servant is legendary, and our young people reflect this disdain for self-sacrifice. The bottom line is expressed in the question, "What's in it for me?" Even these well-orchestrated service events or activities are seen as good for the college resume, to fulfill a graduation requirement, or offer something to share in an interview. It is quite rare to find a youth who sees service as a perspective, an attitude, or simply a lifestyle choice.

When one of the women of the front porch had a son stricken by cancer, it was amazing to see these women go into high gear. They made sure their friend was free to be with her child at the hospital every minute she needed or desired. They coordinated all meals for her family of five, they did the grocery shopping, wash, and made sure her other children got their homework done and to school on time. These women even managed to inscribe our fathers into service. The men cut lawns, served as a chauffeurs, and helped out with any odd jobs that needed doing. For the women of the front porch, this was the expectation and the responsibility of being a good neighbor.

Stories of service to others need to become everyday reports and accounts. We need our youth to regularly hear the chronicling of tales of acts of kindness, generosity, sacrifice, and an acceptance of the role of choosing to serve someone. Service is quite simply the pulse of the genuine good life. Service is both the way and the means of being a good neighbor. Goodness has at its core the daily commitment to being a servant to others. It is our fundamental calling in life.

Called to Significance

"Those who tell the stories rule the world."
— Hopi American Indian Proverb

As a minister, I have sat on literally a thousand plus death beds. At no time did I ever hear anyone facing their final hours, speak of their longing to make more money, do more work, or buy that car or this house, or even to travel to some paradise. Every single time I had the honor and privilege of listening to a person speak to me at the point of departure from this life, what I heard about was a focused need to spend more time with those whim they loved the most, and ironically, the wish to have taken more time to relax and enjoy their days.

So often, I would watch as faces softened, voices dropped, eyes moistened, and the dying soul would reveal a basic yearning to have one more day to be awake, alive, and able to love and forgive.

This is what is meant by significance. It is living with genuine meaning. It is making choices that are not seeking status or worldly success, but rather deciding in favor of being a person worthy of respect and honor. A significant life is a life well lived. It is a balanced life. It is also a life which has created and shown a lot of love and a great will to forgive.

I think we know this. I believe we do. Life is not rocket science. It is not some grand mystery. It's following the heart. It's living the way God intended and hoped. It's making decisions and choices that will please us and God eternally. It's simply being wise.

At every funeral I have ever conducted, maybe with a few exceptions, at some point someone has shared a story that revealed the true nature of the person being memorialized. These stories may move us to tears or to laughter, and they touch our hearts, lift us up, and make us better people. These anecdotes capture the soul of the one departed, and reveal the essential nature of life itself. When folks discuss the funeral, it will be these stories which will be recalled. The prayers, the scriptures read, the hymns sung…those will quickly fall away, but the stories will be around for a long time—maybe forever.

We need to get our young people to understand that every day they're living, they are also dying. Tough lesson, yes, but one God requires us to learn. Our youth must ask themselves what they want to be remembered for. A legacy is never planned in the last weeks of life. A legacy is a collection of choices, a constellation of decisions, a statement of one's priorities.

A legacy is a lifetime process. Our youth need to begin this spiritual journey in their early teens. It will enable them to mature, and enhance the quality of their lives. A life without meaning is empty. It is a waste. It is choosing to be a carcass.

"They tell me we're living in an information age, but none of it seems to be the information I need or brings me closer to what I want to know. In fact, I'm becoming more and more convinced all this electronic wizardry only adds to our confusion, delivering inside scoops and verdicts about events that have hardly begun: a torrent of chatter moving at the speed of light, making it nearly impossible for any of the important things to be heard."
— Matthew Fleming, *The Kingdom of Ohio*

Called to the Same

There is one factor in creating a calling which truly goes against the grain of our American culture. Much of what we are called to do and be is the same for us all. We are not special, or unique. Yes, we may have some significant gifts or talents. Yes, we may have attributes which make us shine, abilities which grab the attention of others, but still, for the most part, our calling is the same.

We are called to love. We are called to accept and forgive and respect others. We are called to seek and at times even find God. We are called to the genuine good life which is only and always about goodness. We are called to bring Heaven to Earth. We are called to live in such a way that we will be remembered fondly. We are called to make a little difference on this earth.

Good stories are all strikingly similar. They are stories which have a common heart and theme. They are gentle, gracious stories which are not only uplifting, at times heart-warming, but also so honest and real we know they are tales worth telling and hearing. These are not just sentimental stories, these are stories which remind us of the risks of loving and living fully, and the miracle of the human spirit to conquer adversity and triumph over tragedy.

These are the sacred sagas crafted out of the wit and wisdom of good folks who make tough choices in tough times and do not shirk God's expectations for them to be at their best. These are the tales of people whose lives reveal an insight, a depth, a purpose, a point, a meaning, a message, a ministry, an attitude, a perspective, a faith and hope and love we wish to never forget.

Stories From Camden

As a youth minister for some forty years, I'm still in touch with many of the young people with whom I worked and loved. When they call or visit, I always enjoy hearing about their lives. Most speak of their busyness, their loves, their travels, and of course, their purchases. They may offer an amusing anecdote, or share a common trend in their days, but for the most part, their words carry the familiar ring of letting me know they are successful. I accept that.

However, there are a few who are different. The difference is one of quality and meaning. The difference is one of spiritual focus. The difference is sensing God's work being revealed through their efforts.

Justin Reilly is a teacher in Camden, New Jersey. Camden is a city with enormous issues and few resources. It is a place where poverty is abundantly present, and education considered a very real challenge. It is not a place where most young white men would choose to teach, let alone live.

I do not want to write a tribute to Justin at this point, as he is still too damn young. I just want to make a single point. Justin is called to teaching. I know this because when he talks to me he tells me stories. He tells me stories about "his kids" and the parents who struggle daily to do a good job. He speaks with such passion and urgency about what he wants for these children.

This past summer he called me to tell me about his plans for his new class. His theme was, "Be a Hero In Your Home Town." He had all kinds of planned events and activities to highlight the theme and bring its powerful message to light. He even had a huge painting of Camden created to inspire and ignite their imaginations. When he told me about his dreams for the year, he could barely catch his own breath. His spirit just flowed. He was on fire.

Every time I talk with Justin, he tells me stories. These stories always reveal his enthusiasm, his energy, and his excitement, and that is the sound of a *calling*. It is not a job. It's a chance to love a bunch of kids. To love them so much and so well that you offer them a taste of hope and the touch of joy. This is how they become "my kids." It makes a world of difference. It will make a world of difference. We need a great many more young folks with a calling!

Story Starters

- What talents or gifts do you possess which almost seem like second nature—they simply come naturally...even easily?
- How do you feel when you are doing nothing? Why?
- Choose a hero of yours and tell a story about this individual that captures their spirit and character.
- What would you consider to be truly significant to accomplish in your life?
- How would you describe your "calling" to date? How have you done in being true to this "calling"?

Section Two

INTRODUCTION

A Good Story Inspires

"Stories have the power to create social change
and inspire community."
— Terry Tempest Williams

"Our chief want is someone who will inspire us
to be what we know we could be."
— Ralph Waldo Emerson

A good story has a spirit and a soul. It is alive. It will grow and shrink, not on demand, but upon reception. A good story is a verb. A story is active, moving and morphing in a million different ways. Stories are always in the process of being transformed—by the storyteller, by the listener, and by God. A good story is also transformational, as if it has hands to shape the human heart.

Stories pick up momentum, and they slow and settle. A good story is infested with mystery and the miracle of life. There is absolutely no controlling a story. It will go its own way and have its way with us.

All good stories are love stories. Though love is not necessarily the topic of every sacred yarn, every story asks us to fall in love with the tale it weaves. Good stories want us to come inside, to feel every inch of their flesh, and to become one with their soul. Good stories yearn to be loved as much, if not more than, they yearn to speak of love as a subject.

A good story needs to be embraced. A story embraces us. A good story is trying to create, trying to plant a seed within our souls and give birth to a new thought, idea, dream, hope, wish, or person. Good stories carry within them a lust for life. They have only one wish, and that is to enable us to fall even more deeply in love with life itself.

The spiritual life is keenly aware that good stories are inhabited by the Holy Spirit, as well as having a spirit all their own. A good story has a force within it. We call this the creative spirit. It simply means that a good story makes things happen. It can ignite love or mercy within us. It can make hope happen. It can be the push we need to jump for joy or make a leap of faith. Good stories wake us up, and get us up, and then seek to lift us up to higher ground.

Good stories are not simply emotional or sentimental. Though they may bank on both, a good story is at work making us mature, stirring up the mystery, and poking and prodding us into movement—being moved, being changed, being transformed.

A good story is like an artist. An artist is seeking to make a point, to highlight a moment of beauty, or offer up a glimpse of grace. The artist hopes to make such an impact that their creation becomes unforgettable. A good story is meant to be remembered, but in the act of remembering it will also change and alter.

Good stories are like atoms, the very stuff of life, and their perpetual movement is one of life's few guarantees.

Good stories. They have a heart. They express a soul. Their spirit proves contagious. They go places we never expected, and inhabit individuals we thought unlikely to be so touched. This is the joy of a story. It is a living thing, and its spirit creates more spirit.

Like love itself, a good story enables us to come alive, and rewards us with the deep satisfaction of knowing and being known. Good stories understand. They show us respect. They demand honesty, and they give it. A good story is indeed a very good friend, a companion of a kind, a source of support and a means of inspiration.

We have been called by God to be co-creators. I believe it is in the sharing of our stories that we most genuinely fulfill this function. The Word of God is God's story. We, God's beloved children, are the sentences, paragraphs, and chapters of God's story. Our stories are created in the image of God. The same Spirit which sparked the Creation is at work in the creation of our stories.

Our stories carry God's signature, and expand our understanding of the heart and mind of God. In our stories, God has declared us to be artists. Our lives are our artwork. God refuses to give us a coloring book page, but rather asks us to create a watercolor of our favorite day—each and every day.

Creating good stories is an art form, and storytelling is the means by which we execute this art, bringing it to life. Our good stories create images of God's Grace. In them, we tell of how we have witnessed the truth, and how we have been informed and formed by a most gracious God.

Our stories create the landscapes of our lives, and reveal the hidden portrait within us. Our stories can be abstract or photo realistic, and can offer an impression or a detailed abstraction.

No matter what the case, our stories shed light on what we find beautiful or ugly, full of wisdom or foolishness, and that which we see as good or bad or even evil. Good stories paint our lives on a living canvas. They witness to the world where and how we believe God has been revealed to us.

In this sense, all stories are both fully human and fully divine.

"We are, as a species, addicted to story. Even when the body goes
to sleep, the mind stays up all night, telling itself stories."
— Jonathan Gottschall

Story Starters

- What do you consider to be the most inspiring book you've read?
- What do you consider to be the most inspiring film you've seen?
- Which story do you find has become a close, personal friend?
- Which story continues to inspire and transform you to this day?
- Which story do you believe animates your soul or informs you of
  your hopes and dreams?

CHAPTER SIX

A Good Story Inspires Love

"Love doesn't just sit there, like a stone: it has to be made,
like bread, remade all the time, made new"
— Ursula K. Le Guin, The Lathe of Heaven

"In our life there is a single color, as on an artist's palette, which
provides the meaning of life and art. It is the color of love."
— Marc Chagall, Chagall

"The giving of love is an education in itself."
— Eleanor Roosevelt

A traditional love story is charming. It may even arouse our passions, but it seldom inspires. Love stories are quite personal and particular to the participants. Even upon listening to the wonders of falling in love, the listener will nod without much emotion or investment, only offering an assurance to the speaker that they have been heard and believed.

But there are exceptions to this rule. At times, someone writes or tells a love story which moves us deeply, even to tears. However, it is not the love which moves us, but the obstacles overcome, or the unlikeliness of the experience in a given situation. Every year there may be one or two good love stories put on film, or expressed in print, but there is a sense that their creation is nothing more than a formula. They seem not quite real and hardly repeatable.

At the end of reading a traditional love story or witnessing one on the big screen, we may feel satisfied or know a moment of sweetness, but there is little spiritual movement—no real inspiration. It may be pleasant, even pleasing, but a traditional love story of two people being swept off their feet by the power of love is, well, just too commonplace.

The love stories which move us and offer genuine inspiration are anything but traditional. They are stories which speak of totally unexpected love, the loving of the very tough to love, the embracing of the outcast, or the courage of loving an enemy.

The love stories which bear the mark of the Spirit are not so much about passion as they are about compassion. It is compassion that reveals the true heart of love. It is compassion which displays the maturity required in loving. It is compassion which lifts the veil on the image of God imprinted upon our souls.

Falling in love is not an art, it is an instinct. Falling in love is the opposite of discipline. It is the surrendering and relinquishment of control. Falling in love is not a craft, a choice, a work. It is simply a response to an intense emotional and spiritual experience. I am certainly not trying to diminish its impact, or its importance, but I am trying to acknowledge that the fall of love makes for a limited story.

I wish to have this chapter speak exclusively to the *art* of loving. I am speaking here of love which is an attitude, a perspective, a way of being, a disciplined doing, and above all else, about a loving which goes against all odds. I wish to explore with you how a good story can inspire loving which is difficult and demanding.

Though I celebrate that love is indeed all there is and that life is not worth much without it, I want our youth to know more about how loving can be a powerful catalyst for healing, hope, and even holiness. These pages will not discuss sentimental love or a schmaltzy story of falling in love. Rather, they will offer up images of the hard work of being an "artist" in loving. It is when loving becomes tough, confusing, complex, even painful, that good stories are written and told.

"In order to create, there must be a dynamic force,
and what force is more potent than love?"
— Igor Sravinsky, An Autobiography

Loving the Tough to Love

"Love and compassion are necessities, not luxuries.
Without them, humanity cannot survive."
— Dalai Lama

Oliver is a guy my father met, and my dad couldn't remember when or where or why they met. He did, however, tell Oliver to stop over some time for dinner with the family. He may not have expected Oliver to do so, but Oliver did just that, and did it every month for several years. Though we never came to know much about Oliver, nor believe much of what he said was his story, we did come to accept Oliver as a regular supper guest in our home. He remains an unforgettable presence in my memories of childhood.

Oliver was bald and only in his thirties. He had circular and thick black glasses. He wore a ton of plaid and always had a bow tie. His clothes were not filthy, but they were soiled. He had bad body odor. He had a loud voice, and an even louder laugh. He was clumsy and had no social graces. He was what my mother called, "a bull in a china shop." To me, he was the guy who ate most of the mashed potatoes and made sure there would be nothing left of desert. He was skinny as a rail, but he ate like a horse. I can't say I ever came to enjoy his company.

My mother came to believe his story was tragic and sad, and she taught my sister and me that we were called by God to be there for Oliver. I now know she had no idea if she was right, but her motherly instincts were in full swing when it came to assessing Oliver's life situation. Mom had decided that Oliver's family had disowned him or certainly had no desire to have anything to do with him. She felt they were still living, but when it came to Oliver, they were in hiding. This made my mom's eyes well up with tears.

She also concluded that he had a very difficult time getting or keeping a job, and he was hungry a lot. She often stated upon his departure that he ate like he had not done so for a week. She also gave him every left over we had, plus a large jar of peanut butter and another of jelly which she stored in the cupboard for his spontaneous arrivals. She would also wrap up a bunch of windmill cookies, which were his favorite. Mom often said that Oliver needed a good woman, to which my father said, "Eve would have been climbing over the hedges of Eden to get out of that deal." Mom would scold Dad, but she would sigh and say it needed to be someone with infinite patience.

Oliver was a monthly regular at our table for four years. Then he just vanished. We think he moved out West. Nobody had any details about Oliver other than our discovery that he walked to our home from Waterford, where he had a small room, which was about twenty miles each way. By the time he arrived, let's say he had worked up a big appetite.

Jesus told his followers that it was no great accomplishment to love the easy to love. I think this meant those we find attractive, charming, carefree, easy to talk to, and who lighten up a room or a table. Oliver was none of those. Oliver was like the arrival of a thunderstorm at a summer picnic. It may not ruin the event, but it sure makes it difficult to enjoy.

It is in loving the tough to love that we mature, and deepen, and become more the people God created us to be. Our youth need to hear stories of such love, love that is service, love that is sacrificial, love that asks us to suffer a bit, even if only in making us uncomfortable. Our youth need to appreciate the transformational power of loving someone who has literally nothing to give back—Oliver had nothing but his appetite to offer.

In four full years and forty-eight meals, we knew nothing about Oliver other than he loved the Chicago Cubs and Bears, was good in math, liked to sing but had an awful voice, and could inhale a whole pie at one sitting. However, we came to see Oliver through my mom's eyes—the lenses of Grace. Mom saw Oliver as a lonely little boy who needed a home and a family and a chance to be loved.

This is what is amazing about a true love story. When the love enables something or someone the world sees as ugly to become quite beautiful. In the flesh, as it did for my mom, or in memory, as it did for me.

Loving the Outcast

Ethel was quiet on the front porch. For Ethel, being this quiet was a miracle right up there with walking on water…or maybe she had the flu. All of the ladies on the front porch realized that Ethel was off. I was listening through my bedroom window, which I often did on hot summer nights without air conditioning, except the occasional breeze off Lake Michigan. I knew something was wrong with Ethel, and I knew whatever it was would be juicy.

After fearless probing, badgering, and a million questions, Ethel broke down in heaving sobs and kept muttering the name of her daughter, Rose Marie. The Greek chorus of porch ladies kept chanting, "What about Rose Marie?" After saying she could not say it about a hundred times, Ethel finally spit it out. "She's engaged!" All the porch ladies gave a rousing affirmation that Rose Marie had found a man, as Rose Marie was one hefty woman, and not all that attractive—not even a pretty face. "She is engaged to a black man named Anthony." The porch went silent. I sat up in bed. In the '50s, this went way beyond juicy.

The quiet, gentle, carefree simplicity of the '50s was a lovely memory for me, but the blatant and vile racism which saturated our whole society at the time (and I suspect still does) was just as strong a recollection. The thought of a daughter marrying a black man was an atomic bomb to the ladies of the front porch. It exploded every hope and expectation, and it left the future in shambles. These women had no consoling words for Ethel, and no way to even begin to process what this would mean for Rose Marie. Most of the ladies had already decided not to tell their husbands and to hide it from their children. This was bad. I mean really *bad*.

Then Charlotte spoke. Charlotte was single, and now fifty years later I am sure was a lesbian, and she had a wild streak in her a mile wide. "Oh, for God's sake, she is just marrying a man of a different color. She could be dead, or maimed, or in prison, or have cancer, for God's sake. Get it together. I mean really, things could be so much worse."

Even I knew Charlotte was wrong. Being dead, having cancer, or even occupying a prison cell would at least secure expressions of comfort and consolation. Choosing to marry a black man would only draw criticism and scorn, and in abundance. The porch conversation swiftly hopped right over Charlotte's blast of reality, and they started asking Ethel about the wedding, which brought on a literal waterfall of tears and anguish. When Ethel asked all of the porch ladies if they would come to the wedding, one could cut the stress-filled silence with a knife. Nobody said anything, and everyone stared off into the blissful neutrality of space. The weeping hit epic proportions.

My mother, Charlotte, and another neighbor Lib all went to the wedding. They dressed to the nines, and brought lovely gifts and cakes for the reception in the basement of the Baptist church. This trio of white women, marinated in the long-held bigotry of our nation, loved Ethel enough to introduce themselves to all of Anthony's family and to give Rose Marie a kiss on the cheek, and to tell her she looked just lovely. They shook Anthony's hand and welcomed him to the "neighborhood family."

Their attendance at the wedding became the stuff of legend in our neighborhood. It was a defining moment for Ethel, who became steadfast in her utter devotion to the three attendees. They would also go to the two baptisms of Rose Marie's two "milk chocolate" children, as my mother referred to them with genuine affection and appreciation for their beauty. To the youth of our neighborhood, these were the women of the future. These were *women with courage and the force of true love. These were the church ladies who actually walked the walk.*

"Do not go where the path may lead, go instead
where there is no path and leave a trail."
— Ralph Waldo Emerson

These days, our youth certainly need to hear stories of courage. Stories which demonstrate the importance of crossing boundaries in order to love those our culture has deemed unfit. Times may have changed since the 1950s, and many outcasts have been brought into the fold, but we all know there remain millions of outcasts waiting to be loved, respected, and accepted.

Who are they in your family, neighborhood, community, church, or nation? Who are the outcasts who are kept from your loving? What are the stories you might tell your children to inspire them to leap the fences of prejudice and possess the courage to welcome someone into their heart?

When was the last time our youth were challenged to knock down a wall, not build another one? How can we help all the "Ethels" in our lives by knowing they have our love and support and courage? How can we help our "Rose Maries" know they are beautiful? How can we defy the power of contempt and disdain and rise up on wings of love and inspire others to do the same?

Loving the Enemy

I was having communion with Archbishop Desmond Tutu of South Africa. I was excited and honored. My friend Lynn Franklin was also the archbishop's publishing agent and good friend, She was hosting him for a week at her home on Shelter Island. The Archbishop celebrates communion every morning, and he was kind enough to allow Lynn to invite several of her friends to join him for the sacrament. As Lynn's pastor, I was a logical choice, and I was delighted to be there.

I truly cannot remember who else was present, but I would say it was a group of about a dozen. The service was informal, but very Anglican, and I felt moved by his presence and his words. It was during the prayers following the sacrament that the Archbishop offered compassionate and even loving words for Osama Bin Laden, who was then still on the run and obviously alive. It was as if the entire group had been spiritually goosed. I could feel many of Lynn's neighbors and friends levitate for a moment, and even I was caught off guard. Yes, I knew we were called to love our enemies, but it felt really risky, stretching love to the breaking point.

At breakfast, which followed our sharing of the sacrament, one of Lynn's friends asked the Archbishop why he had included Osama Bin Laden in his prayers. The Archbishop merely smiled, and said, "Because he is one of God's children and therefore is beloved." I was pretty sure the questioner was thinking, "not my God," but he chose not to further the inquiry.

The directness of Desmond's response spoke of the fullness of his faith. It registered with me this was the same man who brought the power base of apartheid to the table of reconciliation. This was a man of grace. This was a soul who followed Christ, even when inconvenient, or when his whole being may have pulsed with the urge to punish. He offered the hand of love without conditions.

No conditions. Do we have any idea how rare that is?!

Our youth need to hear love stories about how true love is void of conditions. They need to be counseled on the way of grace, a path which does not indulge our need to win, make a point, punish, blame, or harm anyone. Our young people in America are desperate in their need to hear stories of loving which have shed all prejudice and bias.

Many Americans truly struggle with loving the enemy. America is becoming a culture which is far too punitive, elitist, and judgmental. Our self-righteous bravado is contaminating our relationships with the rest of the world and destroying our capacity to be a nation worthy of respect.

Who are your enemies? Who are those who make your stomach turn, your soul wince, and your heart shrink? For whom do you find yourself plotting revenge, or secretly wishing for ways to get even? How do you keep yourself from engaging with or even attempting to know or understand your enemies?

Loving our enemies is hard work. It is also crucial work. It is the love which requires our greatest maturity and faith. It is the love which actualizes a genuine hope. It is the love which is most pleasing to our God. It is a love that is eternal. It is the brick which builds the Kingdom.

Good stories humanize enemies. Good stories enable us to see our enemies are not only human, but potentially friends. Good stories expel the anger and hurt and bias which keep us from caring or knowing compassion. Good stories fill us with the desire to love even when common sense may tell us not to.

Sometimes grace doesn't make sense. It cannot be explained or defended. Grace is that power which shapes us into something better, holier, more alive, more awake, and more fully the creature we were created to be. Good stories are coated in this grace. They call us to love without conditions. They inspire us to be so bloated with love it may spill over…even on our enemies.

The Power of Love

"If there is no communication, then there is no respect. If there is
no respect, then there is no caring. If there is no caring, then there
is no understanding. If there is no understanding, then there is no
compassion. If there is no compassion, then there is no empathy.
If there is no empathy, then there is no forgiveness. If there is no
forgiveness, then there is no kindness. If there is no kindness, then
there is no honesty. If there is no honesty, then there is no love.
If there is no love, then God doesn't reside there."
— Shannon L. Adler

I am not sure if many of our young people these days truly believe in
the power of love. I think not. I think they tend to see love as sentimental
wishful thinking. I find them quite cynical about loving, and they tend
to see it as having limited powers which are often revealed to be bogus.

I cannot even imagine a politician addressing the issue of loving an
enemy or loving those who are in need, are oppressed, the outcasts, or
the victims of our greed and indifference. Love is no longer spoken on
the political stage, and I believe this has much to say about the lack of
ethics we find there.

How would the debate on universal health care change if we were
truly being challenged to love those who have no insurance or coverage?

What would happen in the immigration battle if we were asked to genuinely love the immigrant? How would the issue of gay marriage alter if we were expected to love gay folks as equals? Love does have genuine power. Love is seldom called upon and rarely unleashed.

Love is powerful. It can heal a heart and mind and soul. It can restore confidence and creativity and hope. It can erase a fear, vanquish despair, and help overcome a tragedy. Love can inspire us to take action and make good things happen. Love changes lives. Love bears all things. Love indeed never ends and endures. Love makes all the difference.

Our youth need to know that love alone can make a world of difference. Love is the only means we have to bring us together as one, in harmony, in peace, and striving to take good care of those who are powerless. Love is most powerful when it is called into action. When was the last time you heard such a call?

The Powerlessness of Love

Love is always a risk. It comes with no guarantees, warranties, or certainties. We are never in control of love. We are never in charge.

Love must always risk a loss, an ending, or a betrayal. Love demands surrender to a higher power. Love is in the hands of God. God is the primary source of love.

Stories seem to accept this truth. They are written or told with an understanding that love will have its way with us, and if we are wise, we will allow love to flow into and transform us. Our youth rigorously battle such loss of control. They seek to be in charge of how love plays out. They believe they can write the ending. Our youth need to hear stories that demand them to surrender.

Love is an art. An artist seeks to develop disciplines which help them be better at their craft. Still, what creates a magnificent work of art must go beyond the disciplines of the craft. A true artist reveals the God within. A true artist knows it is the Spirit which determines the flow of the creative act. God remains the ocean into which all love flows.

We are powerless in love. We cannot create it or dominate it or make it happen. We cannot dictate its direction or determine its movements. What we can do is be its willing vessel, a receptacle, a means of transmission. We can open ourselves to receive it. We can take in this love and let it flow through us. We can reflect the image of a God who is Love.

Good stories offer instructions in the art of loving. They tell of love's required disciplines and the work involved in its creation. Good stories tell us how love must grow, widen, deepen, and become stronger, fuller, and more God-like. Good stories claim the fall, trials and tribulations, and triumph of loving. A good story reminds us love will win.

Our youth need to hear and be taught by smart stories which tell the truth of loving. Stories which ask for mature listening and a deep understanding of the demands of grace. Grace is not cheap. The cost of unconditional loving is quite high. Unconditional loving requires a soul which is aware of the centrality of love and a spirit inspired to love those we call our enemies.

Loving in the spirit of grace, without conditions, unafraid of the risks, willing to gamble on loving them our world despises, is as close as we will ever come to the heart of God. Love is how we know God and how God knows us. Love informs us of God's will. It is God's will for humans to be human. We are most human when we love.

"So long as we love we serve, so long as we are loved by others,
I would almost say that we are indispensable."
– Robert Louis Stevenson

Story Starters

- What do you consider to be the hard work of loving someone?
- When have you witnessed love transform someone you found to be quite difficult?
- When were you loved, in spite of yourself, and when you were tough to be around?
- Who are the American outcasts today? What price do we pay for loving an outcast? Share a story of having chosen to love an enemy.
- What conditions do you put on your loving? Why is it vital to love unconditionally?

CHAPTER SEVEN

A Good Story Inspires Mercy

"Teach me to feel another's woe, / To hide the fault I see; /
That mercy I do others show, / That mercy show to me."
— Alexander Pope, "The Universal Prayer"

"The quality of mercy is not strained; /
It droppeth as the gentle rain from heaven /
Upon the place beneath. It is twice blessed— /
It blesseth him that gives, and him that takes."
— William Shakespeare, *The Merchant of Venice*

Of all the stories I have ever heard, and those I have been blessed to tell, my personal favorites are always those which capture the spirit of mercy. These are stories which speak of our humanity and how often we fail to live up to what God and even we expect. They are stories which tell of our incessant need to be forgiven and our pleas for the slate to be wiped clean.

These are sacred stories which reveal God's nature to make the broken whole again. These are the tales of how God inspires us to offer mercy even when our body and soul may ache with the desire for revenge. What

I truly love about these stories is that they are so real, so vital, so vividly revealing of our own human nature.

Mercy is not our nature. It is God's nature. It is a way and path we can choose to take, only when our faith is full and our heart broken and contrite. Mercy is the bold embracing of a forgiveness which truly does forget. Our response to the Grace of God can only be an act of mercy. It is in our acceptance of our own misdeeds, our refusing to love, our resistance to maturing, that we come to know how only God can enable us to show or be shown mercy.

I once heard a story of a young couple who were preparing a supper and enjoying intermittent play with their first-born son. The father was singing a lullaby to his child and tossing him gently into the air. He would catch the boy and draw his giggling body to his chest. It was a game of a kind which every daddy has played with their child. When his wife accidentally knocked a kettle of hot soup on the floor, the distracted young father failed to catch his son, and the infant was killed instantly when he hit the floor.

A fellow minister told me this story, and he went on to speak of the great mercy shown by this young couple and how stunned he had been by their goodness to one another. Each offered full forgiveness to the other. Each refused to place blame, or offer up even a morsel of guilt. This marriage survived the raw brutality of a senseless tragedy, by not compounding the horror by heaping shame upon it. They embraced one another with love, understanding, acceptance, and forgiveness. They never allowed themselves to descend into the abyss of "what if" or "if only." By knowing the fullness of one another's pain, they chose to offer one another the healing balm of grace.

They would go on to have three lovely children and would frequently speak of how the overwhelming loss of their son had become a turning point in their lives and their marriage. Mercy is often the turning point upon which spiritual surrender is declared. Mercy creates faith like nothing else. Mercy beholds the divine. Mercy transforms our soul. Mercy coats us with an eternal awareness of the presence of God.

> "The purpose of human life is to serve,
> and show compassion and the will to help others."
> — Albert Schweitzer

I cherish these stories of pure mercy because they are rare and because they come at times when there is simply no other way. Mercy is born when all else has failed. Mercy is the result of recognizing we are not God, and without God, we have no hope at all. Mercy is such a wild risk and so completely irrational. Mercy is the essence of grace. It is the pulse of God's heart.

Mercy Me

We all rest atop a mountain of mercy. Ironically, most days, we believe ourselves to be seated on level ground. It's just so easy to forget the incredible number of times life and God have forgiven us, our parents, our siblings, and our friends. We have been forgiven by strangers more than we could imagine, and even the earth has shown us mercy. The wise among us know of the mountain. We are fully conscious we have received a daily dose of mercy. Not out of nowhere, but out of an everywhere and all the time God of Grace.

Just as joy goes beyond happiness to a deeper and fuller place of genuine celebration, mercy moves beyond forgiveness to a state of grace. This is the state of believing we have been fully forgiven and granted the goodness of wholeness once again. This is a holy state, a condition in which we become ready to forgive everyone everything. This is a time, an eternal time, of melting into the heart of God.

Mercy is the soil into which our lives are planted. It is a fertile and fragrant soil. Yes, it can be baked hard under the fierce glare of fear. Yes, it can grow the weeds of greed and jealousy and revenge. Yes, it can be strewn with rocks and obstacles of our selfishness and indifference. Still, this soil remains rich and receptive. If worked and watered, it can and will grow much goodness. Mercy is the ground of our being.

Spiritually speaking, we must start with mercy. Eternity bears the promise we will end there as well. Mercy is a circle, a cycle, a never-ending spiral of revealed grace.

The Bully

"But what we can do, as flawed as we are, is still see God in
other people and do our best to help them find their own grace.
That's what I strive to do, that's what I pray to do every day."
— Barack Obama

We hear a great deal about bullying these days. We are baffled
about how our culture came to breed so many cruel and mean-spirited
people…even some children. I believe the catalyst is obvious. It is the
result of a growing absence of mercy in our society. We have become a
nation of blame and punishment. We mock the tender or bleeding heart.
Compassion is neither encouraged nor offered much counsel.

We teach our children to be wary of their neighbor, to look for the
weak spot, or be on guard for their effort to defeat us. Competition has
replaced compassion. We even call upon our children and youth to be
tough and practice tough love. We unconsciously teach them to have
callused hearts. We advocate for souls which will not be played the fool
and often consider mercy to be the ultimate act of a fool—God forbid
we should be "taken advantage of."

Bullies fail to care. They feel little concern and no empathy. They are
heartless. Their souls have shriveled and shrunk to nothing. A bully is
the expression of our society's need to put someone down, to show them

their lack of worth, and to prove the point that they are powerless. It is the lie upon which the philosophy of the survival of the fittest is built. Bullies mistakenly believe they are declaring their superiority.

Bullies mock mercy. They trivialize it and treat it with contempt. Good stories, on the other hand, show bullies for who they really are. A good story never elevates the cruelty of a bully. It does not spotlight or showcase the sadistic pleasure a bully takes in beating up on another person, be it physical, emotional, or spiritual.

Bullies are abusers. Abuse is never the stuff of a good story. Good stories lift up those who challenge a bully to stop. Sacred yarns never place an abuser on a pedestal, but rather focus on those with the courage to take a stand against them. Our young people need to hear stories from those good folks who speak out and up against abuse of any kind.

The fact that bullying has become commonplace and rife in our schools is an embarrassment to our nation. It reveals a deep spiritual need to create young people with tender hearts. We have learned how often the bully becomes the batterer and the molester and the killer. There is no sweet innocence in bullying. It is an attitude and perspective which is void of mercy and thus has no connection to a higher power.

The Wall Maze

"My mission in life is not merely to survive, but to thrive and to do so with some passion, some compassion, some humor, and some style."
– Maya Angelou

Our culture has grown more and more divisive. We are a nation of gated communities. The splits in our society are deep and fierce. Often no contact or communication is permitted, let alone encouraged. Ours is a culture predicated on building walls. Walls to keep out those with whom we disagree, or cannot tolerate, or have deemed unsuitable.

Good stories are about knocking down walls. They tell of courageous folks who took the risk of opening the door to someone thought to be wrong, different, or unworthy. Good stories lift up the importance of celebrating diversity, leading with respect, and the willingness to compromise. Our young people need to hear how opposing views can be reconciled and how opponents can still cooperate with one another. Youth need images of building bridges, and not the endless construction of dividing walls.

In a good story, walls come tumbling down. Somehow, someone manages to create a hole through which mercy can crawl. In a good story, divisions are never celebrated. The goal of life is never to chop it up into fragments. The goal is wholeness. Wholeness is how we become holy. Good stories bring us together, create peace and harmony, and unify. Good stories are never a closed fist, but they are always an open hand.

Mercy Magnified

Most of us, if not all of us, have a story which magnifies our experience and understanding of mercy. It is a moment or memory which allows the concept of mercy to become a reality in heart and mind and soul. It is the time when we felt the presence of God, the God who alone can embrace us with the full measure of grace.

For me, this moment may appear to be quite silly, certainly of little significance in the scheme of things. But I will never forget its impact and the exquisite relief of being shown mercy by my grandmother Othilia Hjortness, a woman notorious throughout our family for not being all that forgiving…even on a good day.

When my grandfather died swiftly and savagely of a heart attack, my grandmother had a horrible time adjusting to being alone. She asked my mother if I would be willing to sleep at her place since we lived caddy-corner from one another. I said no. My mom said yes. Grandma promised to let me listen to the Milwaukee Braves game on the radio as late as I wanted and eat homemade bread in the morning. The bread won.

For three years, on most nights, I stayed over at my Grandma's. Grandma was a stickler for cleanliness, and every night she insisted I take a hot bath before bed. I often pleaded, to no avail, that I was not even dirty. On one such night, post hot bath, I caught a glimpse of my naked self in grandma's huge oval mirror over her dresser. Finding the sight rather exciting, I crawled up on her bed and began to strike a wide variety of poses to observe my naked self.

When Grandma opened the door, I had my legs in the air and was trying to get a good gander of my scrotum. She quickly shut the door. I quickly got into bed and hid myself under the covers. I did not speak to her when she went to bed. She did not say goodnight.

I don't think I slept a wink. I tossed and turned, and I worried Grandma would tell Mom, who might then tell my sister, who might then tell all of my friends, and the nightmare grew worse and worse. Plus, she had seen me naked. I was embarrassed and appalled. My shame was intense.

In the morning, I could barely eat my homemade bread. I wasn't inhaling it like usual. I kept my head down and my mouth chewing. Grandma sat down with her soft-boiled egg and narrow slices of bread for dunking. She sipped her steaming coffee.

Then she spoke.

"Billy, have I ever mentioned to you what a handsome young man you are becoming? My, my, yes you are. In fact, you even have a very handsome body, and the girls will soon be taking notice."

"I sure hope not."

"Trust me—you will change your mind."

"I doubt it!"

Grandma smiled. Then I smiled

Grandma never told anyone, not even my mom. My nude posing remained a secret between us until the day she died. It was a miracle of mercy for me. It was a time when my grandmother had all the power to leave me shattered. She could have made a young boy's life a living hell. Somehow, she knew not to, and chose instead to offer me the message of mercy, which is always expressed in words which carry affection, affirmation, and just a hint of praise . . .

We then chatted about other stuff, and I was swept with the feeling that my whole innards had just had a hot bath. I left for school, but came back and gave Grandma's whiskered cheek a kiss. She thanked me, and never asked why. We both knew why, anyway.

Our young people need to hear such stories, and they need to experience them. They need to pay attention to the signs and sounds of mercy. They need to notice when mercy is being offered or shown. They need to recognize the remarkable gift that is mercy and how it frees us to be whole and hopeful and healed. Mercy is the sound of amazing grace being spoken. Mercy magnifies the priceless grace of God.

Blest Be the Tie That Binds

"Grace is the voice that calls us to change
and gives us the power to pull it off."
— Max Lucado

Ask a gathering of friends, "When was the last time you experienced true mercy?"

I suspect the responses will be slow and awkward and halting. I would bet many folks will look down or away in order to say they have no idea. A few might share. The answers will be cautious and careful, and they will avoid sharing too much intimacy.

Although you might recognize mercy in the tone of what is being said, or hovering near the story or anecdote being offered, you will probably suspect you are not being given the whole truth, and nothing but the truth. You will not be hearing a lie, but you will notice how difficult this truth is to share.

Had the gathering been all adolescents, I doubt you would have heard much of anything. It is highly likely that several youth would ask for the question to be reframed or explained. In fact, most young people are stumped when it comes to comprehending genuine mercy. If I were being asked to explain the question to teens, I would say some things like this:

Mercy is being forgiven for what you know you are truly guilty of. Mercy is when we are offered a free pass by the very one who paid for the ticket. Mercy is when we are given a second and third and fourth and fifth chance. Mercy is when someone chooses spiritually to let go of their very legitimate anger or hurt. Mercy is making the decision to love an enemy.

Mercy is when the mother of a child killed by a drunk driver embraces and forgives that same driver. Mercy is when a couple comes back together after an affair and agrees to trust again. Mercy is when an act of senseless violence is met by an act of loving grace. Mercy is when someone has viciously gotten even and the victim is powerful enough to accept the tie score. Mercy is a home for the homeless, a meal for the hungry, and a coat for the cold child.

The glaring absence of mercy in our American culture has led us to become a nation deeply divided. We are a people incessantly seeking to prove our power. We far too often tend to be unforgiving folks laying blame at the feet of our neighbors. We are a society which does not celebrate diversity, but rather wags a finger at the "fools" on the other side.

Our arrogance is matched only by our ignorance, an inability to recognize that it is only mercy which can hold our hope in place.

A good story never seeks to divide us, or to create a wedge, or build a wall. A good story serves as a bridge over troubled waters. Good stories seek to open lines of communication, remove any obstacles to compromise, and focus us on our common ground. Good stories celebrate our humanity and our equality. Good stories spin a sacred yarn, and this yarn is made of mercy, and is indeed the tie which binds.

Good stories offer our youth a way out of this tangled web of venom and deceit and lies. Good stories point youth to the path of mercy, a way which demands maturity, and expects them to walk the walk. Good stories do not lift up fears and prejudices and vicious hate as a solution. Good stories reveal how grace alone can heal the divide.

"Infuse your life with action. Don't wait for it to happen. Make it happen. Make your own future. Make your own hope. And whatever your beliefs, honor your creator, not by passively waiting for grace to come down from upon high, but by doing what you can to make grace happen...yourself, right now, right down here on earth."
– Bradley Whitford

Story Starters

- Do you believe in forgiving everyone for everything? Why or why not?
- Have you ever been bullied? Have you ever been the bully? What is the relationship of mercy to bullying?
- How can we encourage mercy in our homes, relationships, community, and culture?
- When have you witnessed a wall being broken down, and what was erected in its place?
- Share an experience of mercy from your own life.

CHAPTER EIGHT

A Good Story Inspires Hope

"There is one thing which gives radiance to everything.
It is the idea of something around the corner."
— G.K. Chesterton

"When you say a situation or a person is hopeless,
you are slamming the door in the face of God."
— Rev. Charles L. Allen

"We must accept finite disappointment,
but we must never lose infinite hope."
— Rev. Martin Luther King Jr.

The presence of an absence…at first, I could not truly grasp what this meant, but as I have aged and matured, and hopefully acquired some wisdom, I have come to understand it fully.

Maybe it is simply the result of having to cope with so many losses, but I now possess a good idea about how an absence can take on a life all its own. In fact, at times what is absent in my life is more present than my own life—which is not how it should be, but can be the way it is.

The presence of an absence speaks of a reality when what is missing is so longed for, so yearned after, so deeply desired, that it pulses with a rigorous heartbeat all of its own. An absence may begin to have a voice, a vision, a capacity to motivate and even inspire us. It can also paralyze us with fear or prevent us from maturing.

In our American culture today, and especially within the youthful population, I experience a very powerful absence. It is the almost complete absence of genuine hope. Yes, our culture is saturated with the hope for a better tomorrow, but often this is primarily inspired by the drive for financial or material success, and measures itself solely on the basis of how one is faring economically—the climb up the ladder.

Hope is never about an individual. Hope is never about stuff. Hope is never about money. Hope is seldom, if ever, about success or power or fame. Hope is always about everyone. Hope must be about everyone, everywhere and all of the time.

Hope is when we believe we can and *will* make a difference. Hope is seeking to be significant in the eyes of God. Hope is when we strive to improve our world, to matter, to have lives of deep meaning, and lifestyles that demonstrate a willingness to serve and sacrifice on behalf of others. Hope is fueled by the spiritual power to transform, and this means to change completely.

Hope takes great risks. Hope makes a remarkable leap of faith. Hope expresses God's dreams, and not our own. Hope inspires us to live as if there will be a tomorrow, and that this tomorrow must be a better one for us all. Hope requires maturity. Hope waves the white flag and surrenders to the will of God.

A good story is about those folks who have the courage and wisdom to take a road less traveled. They follow the beat of a different drum. They do not seek to impress anyone, nor do they aspire to greatness. These are the stories of folks with integrity and dignity who offer up their talents and gifts as a sacrifice to better humankind. These are the folks who wish to build the Kingdom of God on this earth and in this time.

Hopelessness

"In the face of uncertainty, there is nothing wrong with hope."
— Bernie Siegel, Love, Medicine, and Miracles

After the slaughter of innocent children in Sandy Hook, CT by a clearly mentally unstable young man, there was a concerted effort to ban assault weapons. An assault weapon has no other purpose than to kill people. Seventy-five percent of the public approved. We could not get the ban, as the other twenty-five percent had the lobbying dollars to block it in our "marching in place" Congress. This made me and many others, maybe even you, feel hopeless.

Several young, unarmed black men have been shot by white police officers. At first, everyone sought to show respect for our police and their public service. However, for white folks like me, it has become increasingly apparent that had these young men been white, they would not be dead. A young black man is eight times more likely to go to prison for the exact same crime committed by a white—this makes me feel hopeless, as if racism continues to win over and over again.

I have worked with adolescents for forty years, and have often been asked to help wrestle with the despair created by adolescent depression or suicide. The numbers are staggering. I suspect that a good many of our young traffic deaths are also suicides. In a culture which keeps calling these the best years of our lives, I feel hopeless in the wake of so many teens choosing to end it all.

These are some of the recent events which have popped my hope bubble. They have provoked my fear and fueled my anger. Yes, they probably speak to my own personal bias and concerns as well as reveal some of my political prejudices. Still, the hopelessness is real, and I search daily to find ways out of this despair.

The hopelessness I observe most frequently in our youth is the erosion of their belief they can make a real difference. This is coupled with an ever-growing greed which contaminates their morality on every level. When young people stop believing they can help make the world a safer and saner and simpler place to live, a planet which is cherished and protected, and a population which truly celebrates its diversity and its equality, then they easily become addicted to money and "stuff."

If there is a crisis in America, it is this. What will it be like to witness a nation whose youth know few hope-filled stories, and have none to tell their children? What will life be like when all hope is gone, drained off and away, and sailing off to the sewer? It will look like Hell, and Hell is the opposite of the very Kingdom we are called to create. Hell will be the dead silence created by the absence of all good stories. Dead silence is the elimination of hope.

Finding Hope

"If we were logical, the future would be bleak indeed.
But we are more than logical. We are human beings,
and we have faith, and we have hope, and we can work."
– Jacques Cousteau

First, let us acknowledge that hope comes not from the outside in, but from the inside out. Hope is a function of the soul and what our heart absorbs from this life of ours. Hope requires a receptive soul, one open to receiving the Word of God.

The Word is ife. The Word is our own lives. The Word is God's story. The Word is our stories. The Word is the language of the soul. It is often expressed only in sighs and whispers and dumbstruck moments of genuine clarity and awe. It is the soul which keeps us humble, and it is humility that will remind us we did not create hope—we can only create a context conducive to its growth.

Our souls know when hope is being witnessed, and this is why our souls develop radar-like ability to locate stories which speak to the human need to be transformed. The soul knows where to look and when to listen. The soul knows why stories can be sacred and what makes a story eternal. The soul knows how to discover, uncover, and recover those tales which tell the gospel truth.

Our modern lives are often chaotic, governed by unproductive busyness and the pursuit of the trivial and short-lived. The soul can be silenced, but until such time, it will chant of its need for us to pay attention to that which ultimately concerns in life. The soul seeks stories of mercy, justice, grace, peace, equality, and the divinity revealed within humanity. The soul winks and points at the flawless goodness revealed by the stories of ordinary folks with extraordinary faith.

"Patience is the art of hoping."
— Vauvenargues

The soul knows the real work of hope, the incredible patience required, and the necessary determination and drive. Hope is received by the wise, those who know life is not about doing better, but being smarter. Hope comes to those who wait. Hope comes to those who have pried open their hearts and minds and spirits, and they let in the vision and voice of God. Hope is found by those sweet souls who know to look for God in the most unexpected places. True hope is not hidden, it is just seldom noticed. Like the religious leaders on the road to Jericho who ignored the battered man at the side of the road, we are too busy to pay attention.

Living in Hope

"In every winter's heart there is a quivering spring, and behind the veil of each night there is a smiling dawn."
–Khalil Gibran

Hope is a perspective. Hope is an attitude. Hope is a way of being. Hope is a choice of doing that which the soul feels called to do. Hope is obedience and following a higher power—God as you understand God. Hope is a lifestyle. Hope is a path, a road, a journey, an adventure, a quest, a destination. Hope moves forward. Hope is an eternal spiral upward. Hope is the dirt of higher ground.

Hope dictates a whole new set of values. It is the formation of an ethical framework, and the actualization of our faith. There are few of us who have managed to live our own God-given truth. We may have done it for a time, or on an occasion, but most of us fail to sustain the spiritual energy and maturity required to be grounded in truth.

Few of us are able to create hope-filled lives on a daily basis. This takes substantial maturity and courage, and it requires a well-nourished soul. It is a worthy ideal, but a road less traveled. We need to take this journey, and our youth need to learn of this "other" way.

Good stories almost always offer us insight about those who live in hope, even for a day. Living in hope means to choose to be wide awake, fully aware, and engaged in receiving the day. Living in hope is the belief we can make a difference and then making it happen. Living in hope is when we make decisions which reflect our obedience to God's will. A life spent in the pursuit of hope may not be called a success, but it certainly earns the label of being significant.

Christopher was twelve years old and had brain cancer. I had been called by his parents that morning, as the fast-growing tumor had just taken away his sight. As I drove to the hospital a good hour away, I kept asking myself what on earth I could say to this courageous young boy. I certainly could not pretend he would see again, and I assuredly would not offer him any false hope. Somehow, I had to speak to him about being blind, but I would need to do so on his terms.

I reluctantly entered his hospital room. Christopher looked in my direction and asked if it was me. He told me his mother had said I would be coming. I took a deep breath and told him we needed to talk. He agreed, but he had something to tell me first. This is what he said: "Pastor Bill, I need a computer that works with braille, and I want you to find out if there are ten speed tandem bikes. That way, my friends can steer and ride up front, and I will be the leg power in the back. Can you do those things for me?"

Christopher would die before I would find out the answer to either of his inquiries. However, I was deeply moved by this young man's remarkable capacity to cope with his cancer. Christopher taught me that there is no such thing as false hope. All hope is hope. Hope is alive as long as it is being chosen. Hope is what animates the soul in face of horrid, even impossible odds. Hope chooses life even when all else fails—including the human body.

Christopher lived hope until his last breath. All who were blessed to have known him in his last days were deeply touched and transformed by his will to have one more day. His hope was passionate and burned brightly until the bitter end. At no time was he willing to surrender his hope. He carried it aloft and kept moving forward and upward to higher ground—to a heaven where they have braille computers and ten speed tandem bikes.

Christopher's life and death is a good, even great, story. It is one we need to tell often, and thereby remind young people of just how precious life can be, and how amazing it is to choose to be hopeful. This story is not a downer. It is not too sad to tell. It is the kind of story which opens up the soul, jars the spirit loose, and enflames the human heart with a passion for being alive.

A Slogging Hope

Hope isn't always pretty. It can be painful and brutally demanding. It often requires a good bit of suffering and forces us to confront life's ugliness. Hope is born of courage, and courage, as we know, is not the absence of fear, but the willingness to move on in spite of our fears. The courage of hope is crucial.

Hope is created by a heart which is willing to be cut wide open. Hope is the offspring of a bleeding heart. There can be no hope without first embracing life on life's terms, and those terms are about slogging, moving forward with diligence, and a steadfast commitment to meet the day head-on.

Slogging is the substance of a life lived in hope. Slogging speaks not to a charmed life, or an easy existence, but of the hard work of loving and forgiving. Slogging seldom receives recognition and rarely earns fame or fortune. Slogging is getting through and getting by. Slogging accepts the frequency of critique, judgment, indifference, apathy, and even hate.

Sloggers are those who understand that hope is hard won. Good stories are filled with the tales of sloggers, those good folks who display great integrity in how they conduct their lives. A slogging hope is a tremendous statement of trust, a basic belief that spiritual obedience will lead us home to God.

Creating a Climate of Hope

Hope is an atmosphere. Hope is an aura. Hope is a climate and a context. Hope is the setting in which we must choose to believe or be afraid, create or destroy, live or die, inspire or become cynics, and is a crucial aspect of what rounds us out. Good stories speak to us about how hope enables us to live good lives and to build the Kingdom of God in the here and now. Without hope as the central message, a story has little to nothing to say. The blood, sweat, and tears of hope beat at the heart of a vast majority of the best stories we hear in a lifetime.

Have you ever wondered why we rise to the occasion during tragedy? Why is it that we show our true colors when we are hit by life's very real adversity? It is because our core is the soul. We are grounded in God's Grace, and when all of our attention is focused, we are capable of doing and being great things—great in the eyes of God.

"Hope is the thing with feathers that perches in the soul."
— Emily Dickinson

I took my youth group from Shelter Island to the Simon Wiesenthal Center in Los Angeles. The kids were not thrilled about being dragged away from the intrigue and fascination of Hollywood, Westwood, and the beaches of Santa Monica. They were dazzled by the world of movies and could not get enough of star gazing. The trip to the Wiesenthal Center was being treated as an obligation, a must do, a chore, something to tell parents in order to make the trip sound worthwhile. To be honest, I sort of felt the same way, but I hoped the experience would be at least somewhat memorable. Memorable it was.

Our visit was filled with educational exhibits and experiences, each challenging us and confronting us with the atrocities committed by our fellow human beings. It was sobering, strong, and explosive. One had to feel and think deeply, and there was no doubt we'd leave untouched or unchanged. The photos from the Nazi concentration camps were arresting and overwhelming. Stuffing our neighbors into ovens, or gassing them in mass in supposed shower rooms, was difficult to swallow or comprehend. "How could this have happened?" was the unspoken echo of the Center. It was the message of the place and the memories it housed.

During the course of our tour, I was stopped by a guide who informed me that a woman, a survivor of Auschwitz, was willing to meet with our group—would we be interested? I was thrilled. I was anxious. Did I want our young people to know? Did I want to know? I had never heard a survivor speak. What would it be like? How would it impact us? How would we recover for the rest of our jam-packed trip? I knew the questions were stupid, so I gave an immediate yes.

I cannot recall her talk in detail, and I have long since forgotten her name, but her story went something like this:

She was sent to Auschwitz when she was sixteen. She told us how her friends from school smirked and smiled maliciously as she was identified for transportation. She talked of being stripped naked and showered and de-loused. She spoke of how they slept six to a platform of wood and how they all needed to turn at the same time, and if one got up to use the bathroom, everyone would have to stay awake until they returned. She offered hideous *stories of the food and their treatment by the guards. She sighed deeply as she explained the day she knew she would never see any of her family again.*

She also told us of the goodness and courage and grace she experienced in Auschwitz. She wove wondrous tales about how they prayed together, sang together, and nursed each other back to health. She mentioned with a laugh how they fasted during the high holy days, giving up their gourmet bit of bread or tin of thin soup. She offered insight after insight about how they created a climate of hope in one of the darkest places ever created on earth.

How? By being kind, showing compassion, caring, being concerned for one another, and most of all, by being together even in the bleakest of despair. They chose not to lose faith. They chose not to surrender their souls. They withheld their spirits, by holding hope close to their hearts. Hers was not a story of survival. It was a story of how creating a climate of hope in the midst of evil enabled them to live and die in dignity.

The kids left the Wiesenthal Center in silence. This was a story which had marked their souls forever. It had spiritually impacted their heart and touched their spirits. They were a bit wiser, gentler, and yes, more faithful. Our youth knew hope on this day, its ragged, disheveled dirty side, its remarkable ability to shine in the darkness, and the impossibility of destroying it in humans so inspired by life. I don't think any of us have forgotten this sweet, gentle, funny, and engaging lady with the wide smile and warm wit who told us a story of how a climate of hope cannot be destroyed, even by evil. We were transformed by her sacred story.

Every victim of the Holocaust has a story to tell which needs to be heard. Until our young people listen to those who have truly suffered and lost, they will never mature. Our young need to feel empathy for those who have known great anguish, or endured hideous atrocities, or been made into the innocent victim. This empathy will free them to become spiritual and allow their souls to rise and fly. It will offer them a faith which bleeds with a deep respect for the pain they have known first-hand.

Hope swims in a sea of blood. This is not a pleasant image. It is, however, the truth—the gospel truth.

Hope and Death

"Hope is not the conviction that something will turn
out well but the certainty that something makes
sense, regardless of how it turns out."
– Vaclav Havel, *Disturbing the Peace*

I love the tradition of a wake. I am not sure why it's called a wake, but I suspect it must have something to do with being awakened to the value of the life lost. I love the reverie of a wake, the celebrating, the eating and drinking, and the raucous telling of stories.

These are the true stories of a life. They are fact and fiction, poetry and prose, myth and gospel. These stories are stirring, ribald, tender, and tough. These stories swirl about the wake like the chaos before the Creation, and in that same spirit, create a zest of a new beginning. A wake is neither somber nor reverential. It is an explosion of love, and everyone walks away having been hit by some of the spiritual shrapnel. It is a mess, but a Holy mess.

I love a wake because it is so hopeful. It's so amazing to watch folks bring a soul back to life for a few hours. The spirit of a wake is pure resurrection. It is like a balloon released without having been tied off, and it zooms about wildly in every direction. A wake is not a religious ceremony, but a spiritual event. A wake never stays in the lines of protocol or order. A wake dances, and there is no *real* dancing which has to follow footprints on the floor.

When I was an intern pastor at Holy Communion Lutheran Church in Racine, WI, my first funeral was for a young man who had been swept into Lake Michigan with three of his friends during a surprise April snow squall. The four had been playing "beat the waves," but they were captured by a savage and huge second wave.

The friends of this quartet attended four funerals in a week, and when I met with them briefly at a park where they had regularly hung out and where a plaque was installed to commemorate the four boys, they spoke honestly about hating the funerals. They said the funerals seemed to be talking about four guys they did not know. What they longed for was to tell the true stories of their friends.

I have never forgotten their stern and strong message. Funerals need to be about the souls of the departed, not a religious ceremony which speaks only of the virtue of the Church, and the false "sainthood" of the deceased. There is no hope in a hollow ceremony. The hope comes when we free the spirit of the dead to be alive again, and speak to us, seize us by the throat, and throttle us with its abundant but simple truth.

Death does not extinguish hope—at least it should not. Death can ignite hope. Death offers a fierce focus on life and demands we know its value. Hope is what emanates from the stories told of a loved one lost. These stories are eternal. They are woven out of holy cloth. These stories are the fire in our hearth, each one kindling, each one dry and ripe to blaze.

Our youth need to hear these stories spun from sacred yarn. They need to learn the vital art of remembrance. The maturity and spiritual depth of our young are dependent on them being taught to remember, to remember well, and it is our job as adults to offer them daily lessons on the discipline of recall.

"Every parent is at some time the father of the unreturned prodigal,
with nothing to do but keep his house open to hope."
— John Ciardi

Story Starters

- Offer a definition of hope.
- Why is true hope almost always about everyone and not just the individual?
- Share a story of a time when you felt hopeless. How did you work your way out of the situation?
- When have you offered someone a story of hope or inspired one?
- How can we choose to create a climate of hope?

CHAPTER NINE

A Good Story Inspires Joy

"If you are alone, tell some stories to yourself. This is a different kind of pleasure, and it has, indeed, its reward. I have tasted a little of everything, I have truly never enjoyed anything more."
– Charles Nodier

"Joy seems to me a step beyond happiness—happiness is a sort of atmosphere you can live in sometimes when you're lucky. Joy is a light that fills you with hope and faith and love."
– Adela Rogers St. John, *Some Are Born Great*

"One filled with joy preaches without preaching."
– Mother Teresa of Calcutta

I believe joy is transcendent. Joy lifts us up and reveals the divine within us. Joy is what can happen when the soul is free to fly on the wings of faith and hope and love. Joy isn't other worldly, but it does completely transform this world. Joy unites us with everyone, everywhere. Joy is the glue of grace.

It is not that joy is better than happiness, it is simply different. Joy is all about "we" and happiness primarily about "me." Joy is a process. Happiness is a point. Joy contains suffering and embraces it. Happiness leaps right over it. Joy is a test. Happiness is a quiz. Joy is the presence of God. Happiness is the presence of, well, happiness.

Joy is different in its intensity, focus, and purpose. Joy is brilliant. It is laser focused. It is a moment of feeling at one with life and God. Joy is when we have stopped orbiting and landed in our lives. Joy is when we have come home to God as we understand God. Joy is when we understand how deeply we belong, how connected we are, how bonded by sorrow we are, and yes, joy itself. Joy is when we are completely congruent. We are exactly who we were meant to be.

The possibility of joy gets us up on many mornings!

Ordinary Joys

"The joy that is felt at the sight of a new-fallen snow
is inversely proportional to the age of the beholder."
— Paul Sweeney

I took a group of adults on a weekend retreat to a great Inn in New Preston, Connecticut. As we drove down the road by the lake to the inn, it began to snow—huge, jumbo, Goliath flakes. We all hushed and sighed. It was lovely, like being on the inside of a snow globe. We got out of our cars, and one of the women said, "Let's go to bed now, I can't wait to see what this will look like come morning." We all laughed and agreed.

In the morning, it was a visual wonderland. Every nook and cranny of the earth was coated in four to six inches of fresh, powdery snow. The sun was bright and the world shimmered and sparkled. Everywhere we looked was more glorious than the last. We all walked to the inn's main house for breakfast, and we oohed like little kids who just realized they had a snow day home from school. The same lady said, "I don't mean to say I told you so, but I told you so."

Our day was spent playing in the snow, building snowmen, making snow angels, and driving down country roads that felt like winding through icicle caves. We went to a local restaurant for soup and a sandwich and immediately noticed it was packed. We asked our waitress if they were always this busy. She said, "Oh no, it's just that everyone is out enjoying the snow. No matter how many times we see it...well, it's still a miracle, don't you think?" We agreed, and slurped down our steaming hot soup.

Many of life's joys are commonplace. It's just a matter of whether or not we are ready to receive them. A sunrise or sunset, a snowfall, fall foliage, tucking a child in at night, reading that child a bedtime story, sitting quietly with a soulmate and sipping wine and sighing, and the list could go on and on and on. There are many ordinary events which yield extraordinary joy. If our soul is receptive and our heart opened wide, these events have the capacity to reveal the eternal. They are heaven brought to earth, plain and simple.

"People from a planet without flowers would think we must be mad
with joy the whole time to have such things about us."
— Iris Murdoch, A Fairly Honorable Defeat

Tidings of Comfort and Joy

Many of us truly enjoy Christmas. Even some of us who do not believe in Jesus and who observe different holy days with other religious rituals and traditions can still be moved by the magic of Christmas.

Christmas is a time heavily laden with stories. I cannot begin to recall just how many good Christmas stories I have heard over the years; this is why finding my youth group mute on the subject was so frustrating. The real magic of Christmas is its ability to inspire good stories.

The Christmas spirit offers tidings of comfort and joy. There is comfort and joy to be found in abundance within this spiritual reality— we are God's beloved children. We are held close by this God. We matter to God. We are thought of with the same love and affection that we feel for our own kids.

> "A good conscience is a continual Christmas."
> — Benjamin Franklin

Whether it's Christmas or the holy days you celebrate, they are filled with images of what we long for and wish for the rest of the year. These holidays are made holy by their incessant effort to reignite the human spirit to pursue the divine Spirit. At this splendid time of year, we create stories worthy of sharing. Stories which hold within them the profound wish of a Christmas to bless us everyone.

If it feels like Christmas, right this very minute, then joy is hovering nearby. Stories which capture the Christmas spirit of graciousness, generosity, peace, justice, and the love of family and friends, even the extravagant love of an enemy, are not just good stories, they are gospel stories, and they write a fifth gospel upon the human heart.

Listen up! There are always the sounds of Christmas joy in the air. They are the echo of amazing grace.

Heather, my son's wife, chose to work on Christmas day. She works with children who are autistic or have suffered brain injuries. Heather had noticed during the weeks leading up to Christmas that the children were asking the staff members where they would be for Christmas. Almost every staff member stated they would be home with family. Heather saw how wounded this left the kids. Once again, these kids had to face the grim reality that they would not be home for Christmas. They would not be with their families for a myriad of reasons.

Heather chose to go to work that Christmas. She made a big breakfast for all the kids, brought movies to watch, games to play, and excitedly watched the kids open their gifts.

One eight-year-old boy was clutching his final gift from Santa and refused to open it up. Heather asked him why. He said that for eight years Santa had forgotten him, and he just wasn't sure if Santa knew him well enough to get him what he wanted—headphones. Knowing Santa had done just that, she encouraged the boy to open his final gift. Heather said looking at his face was just like swallowing Christmas.

Joys = Blessings

Here is one surefire way to gather good stories with your children, youth, family, or friends. Have each person write a list of blessings. I think you will be pleased to see how these lists are seldom about material goods, money, popularity, prestige, or power. The lists will be plain and simple. They will contain the names of loved ones and cherished friends. They often will list opportunities for growth and maturation, as well as challenges faced and met. They will note health and one's state of being. They often refer to God in a powerful way, revealing an intimacy which might not normally be claimed.

When we live, share, tell, remember, or write down our blessings, we feel a sense of joy. Not a burning bush of radiant joy, but a low steady burn, like a candle at a window in winter, guiding us home. This joy stems from experiencing the blessings all over again. This time we can take the time to savor it.

> "The hardest arithmetic to master is that
> which enables us to count our blessings."
> — Eric Hoffer, *Reflections on the Human Condition*

Enjoyment

When a parent has the courage to ask me what they might need to improve upon to be a better parent, I always say the same thing: enjoy them! So many children in our modern world are treated as if they are burdens. They know it, sense it, and feel it. They are often burdens, but it is because we have made them so.

We clutter their lives with so much to do that we must become their chauffeurs, personal chefs, assistant coaches, guidance counselors, tutors, and spiritual mentors. We want them to do it all, and so we, too, must do it all. We resent it. They resent it. It's a rat race run on a leash.

I have heard so many damn excuses about why our children and youth are so busy, and none of them make the remotest sense. There is no time for our kids to relax or just be children. There is little time for them to re-create. They are incessantly on the go, worshipping at the god of being busy, and complaining bitterly of having no time. These young people are already weary.

Parents speak of their children's accomplishments as if they were just back from war. Life was never intended to be a battle for grades, SAT scores, popularity points, athletic honors and accomplishments, and a host of extracurricular activities for which we say, "Keeps them out of trouble." Maybe it does, but it also keeps them away from having or knowing their own soul. It keeps us away from getting to really know them and them getting to know us.

The whirlwind lives of today's kids seldom yield joy. Joy is slow and patient and must be savored to be appreciated. Why are we proud of weary kids and youth? Why are we proud of our children doing three, four, or five hours of homework a night? Can it possibly be healthy for our youth to be on the go from eight o'clock in the morning until ten or twelve at night? Is it any wonder they seek joy in, oddly enough called, recreational drugs or sex?

There is no such thing as a good story which tells us about someone's busyness. This is called complaining, bragging, defending, or explaining. Is there anything more boring than hearing someone drag on and on about how worn out they are? Still, it's a reality which dominates many conversations. We still tend to believe our importance to be measured by our busyness. What it really measures is a profound lack of enjoyment in our lives.

Joy Is a Moment

I have known happiness for a few days at a time. I have had some excellent weeks filled with beauty and hope and a sense of awe. Rarely have I known a month or two when life simply felt easy, filled with the aura of raw joy. I have never been lucky enough to know a full year when joy was the dominant theme.

For me, joy comes in moments—a glimpse or glance of grace now and then, a stunning epiphany or revelation, a morsel of time that takes my breath away and leaves me dumbstruck. These are moments when time stands still. We are able to see inside the event or experience, and we can hear its message—the Word of God echoing off its walls. Joy leaves a mark, the signature of the presence of the Spirit.

These tiny moments have a huge impact on our days, our lives, and even our relationships. These magnificent moments get us in touch with our longings, our yearnings, and our deepest desires. They are sparks which ignite the soul, and they illuminate the wishes of our hearts. Moments of joy leave us wanting more, more of life. What is most amazing is that we want it on God's terms and not on our own.

"Seize from every moment its unique novelty.
And do not prepare your joys."
— Andre Gide, Nourritures Terrestres

Joy Is a Choice

I believe it is the will of my Higher Power for me to have joy in abundance. I would contend the God I believe in wishes me joy each and every day. I also believe when we choose to enjoy the day, we are offering joy to God.

Joy is indeed a choice. We know this, but ironically seldom take note of it, nor do we pay much attention to its infinite possibilities. We are called each day to notice when, where, and how joy is being served up to us.

Joy is a perspective, a way of seeing and being, and a spirit. It is not only a style of life, but it can be the manner in which we conduct our lives. When we see life through the eyes of joy, we not only seek out the best in the day but also in ourselves and others. We become not only a positive force but also a productive one.

There is one surefire way of capturing stories of joy in our daily lives. Pay attention to the body of knowledge we have available. Our bodies will point out joy. The lump in the throat, the goosebumps, a shiver up and down the spine, having our breath stolen from us, and being moved to tears, our bodies are on the ready to inform us when joy is hovering nearby.

A beloved therapist who served as clergy showed me another, even more practical way to hunt down moments of joy. Trust me, he had ample clients. His name was Lloyd Rediger.

Lloyd gave me a stack of blue 3 x 5 notecards and told me to write down anything positive or enjoyable or made the day brighter. These cards were imprinted to look like an actual doctor's prescription form. I thought this was about the hokiest idea I had ever witnessed. He then told me to tape the cards to a mirror or space I saw on a frequent basis.

About six months later, having chosen to be obedient, since whatever I had been doing sure wasn't working, I noticed the mirror over my dresser was totally blue. I stood and read them all out loud, a ritual I would continue for the remainder of my time with Lloyd. It would become one of the most significant learning experiences of my life, and it certainly made me conscious of my capacity to make good, healthy, and even joyful choices on a daily basis.

Good stories are just like those blue prescription cards. They tell us how joys can be contagious, and inspire us to make wise choices. No, we are not in control of joy, but we have the capacity to create a context conducive to joy showing up on a regular basis. We have the prescription in the palm of our hand and simply need to fill it.

Story Starters

- Share a favorite memory of a moment filled with joy.
- Share a story of having witnessed the joy of a friend, neighbor, or complete stranger.
- When was the last time you truly and fully enjoyed being you?
- Who is the one person you most enjoy spending time with? Why?
- Write yourself a prescription for joy.

CHAPTER TEN

A Good Story Inspires Faith

"Stories require faith, not facts."
— T. A. Barron

"Faith is like radar that sees through the fog—
the reality of things at a distance the human eye cannot see."
— Corrie Ten Boom, Tramp for the Lord

All I have seen teaches me to trust
the Creator for all I have not seen."
— Ralph Waldo Emerson

Faith is a verb, not a noun. Faith is a question, not an answer. Faith is always seeking, but never fully arrives. Faith is a deed, not a creed. Faith is never organized, and always a bit of a mess. Faith is spontaneous, not predetermined. Faith is the opposite of fear. Faith has no need for cynicism. Faith is wise, but never a know-it-all. Faith is never certain, and remains coated in mystery.

Faith is alive. Faith cannot be indoctrinated, only inspired. Faith is a not a ritual or routine, but rather a rite of passage. Faith concerns us ultimately and avoids all trivial pursuits. Faith is a pilgrimage toward a higher power, and it includes no ladder to climb—faith is completely void of hierarchy.

Faith is a paradox. It remembers always, and ceaselessly pursues its present desires and future dreams. Faith is a longing lived, and a radical acceptance of dying. Faith refuses to stop exploring and yet often settles on playing the hunch. Faith is not arrogant or proud but is critically humble. Faith is a genuine force, a unique power, but it is also most willing to serve and sacrifice. Faith is holy and human. Faith is now and eternal.

Faith is both living and dying at all times. Faith is passion and compassion. Faith can never be explained or proven or duplicated, and yet it can be claimed. Faith moves in circles, and yet it is always spiraling upward and downward. Faith is lost and found every moment of every day. Faith is given by a gracious God who promises we will do and be greater than the Giver.

Faith is found in stories. Faith can only be expressed in the living stories we call our histories. We are called by faith to learn our stories, share our stories, listen to those of others, pay attention to stories we suspect to be written by God, and tell our stories in truth—a gospel truth. Only a story can capture the heart and soul of faith.

In a very real way, these stories make up the fifth gospel we write with our lives—our sayings and sermons, healings and miracles, and how we have navigated the passion narrative of our existence. These stories are our psalms and proverbs and parables. They are our testimony. They give structure and shape to what we hope will be our legacy.

There is not a single aspect of life that does not have a story to tell. Under the right circumstances, and to the right audience, every day has lessons to teach, revelations to reveal, miracles to offer, and mysteries to ignite. We must open up our kids to looking to their very own days to find meaningful stories. Stories need not be ancient to be of value, nor to possess wisdom. Our own stories have much to teach and reveal about God.

We need to get rid of the notion that a good story must sound religious to be of spiritual benefit. Some of the best stories of our lives may be far too radical or raw or dark for airing in a parish sanctuary. Some of these good stories are so simple and so direct they hardly sound worthy of claiming the involvement of God...but they are! Good stories come out of life, and all of life is soaked in the presence of God.

"We couldn't conceive of a miracle if none had ever happened."
— Libbie Fudim

The Garden of Faith Stories

"The more help a person has in his garden, the less it belongs to him."
— William H. Davis

Faith stories begin in a garden. The garden is a name for paradise. Paradise is created in the image of Heaven. Paradise knows no Hell. Even the serpent is a welcome guest. All gardens are plots of land, or in the case of our faith stories, the ground of our being.

I like the image of dirt. I love that faith stories are dirty. They must contain a deep and tangled web of roots, numerous wily worms, and be fertilized with life's assorted messes. Faith stories should never be treacly sweet.

A good story garden must battle a bumper crop of weeds: arrogance, ignorance, self-righteous pride, materialism, greed, and the curse of selfishness. Most good gardens need fencing or a scarecrow for protection from that which would devour it.

A good gardener pays attention to their garden. They nourish the garden with the waters of stillness, silence, solitude, prayer, worship, study, and devotion. They weed the garden by acts of service and sacrifice and even suffering. They protect the gardens by creating true friendships, families, and communities.

Faith stories will blossom with the careful preparation of the soil and the planting of seeds. The seeds of faith stories are compassion, courage, maturing, kindness, generosity, graciousness, mercy, awe, and wonder. Our faith stories are like a garden of carefully crafted vegetation—row upon row of goodness.

We must trust these stories to emerge. They will naturally, and by divine sanction, wind their way to the top, and burst the ground with their beauty. They will be fragile for a time. They will need proper nourishment from the sun and water. Significant weeding may be required from time to time, though some of the weeds will ironically be just as lovely.

I guess as I write this, I am realizing that a story garden must be both wild and tame, and that balance is, as always, the key. We gardeners must know when a story should blossom and give forth its own fruit, and when we must nudge it along and help it survive until its fecundity is secure. We must be wise to know when we must step back and when we are being called to step in. Stories do have lives of their own, but as their tellers, we bear responsibility for their ultimate beauty.

Think of your soul as a garden of stories. Your soul requires the fencing of peace and quiet to be creative. Your soul must be watered by beauty and love and hope and the sunlight of mercy. Your soul must work. It must do gardening. It must weed and watch and become in tune with what our blossoms require to thrive. Our souls must be unafraid to dig down deep into the very core of our beings and unafraid to be coated in the grime of self-discovery and maturing. A soul is wise and understands that a gardener never has clean hands.

"More things grow in the garden than the gardener sows."
— Spanish proverb

When Heaven Comes to Earth

"Aim at Heaven and you will get Earth thrown in.
Aim at Earth and you get neither."
— C.S. Lewis

A majority of good faith stories offer up images of when heaven comes to earth. These images reveal our personal conceptions of Heaven not necessarily as a place or a people, but as a state of being. In other words, good stories seek to express the inexpressible. They strive to point out the presence of God in our midst. They search for those moments when we truly experience our souls maturing, our hearts bursting, our minds being blown away, and our lives being utterly transformed.

Somehow, we seem to know Heaven when we see it or hear it or are touched by it. When we are choosing to be awake and aware, we are able to fully engage its mystery, embrace its miracles, and be embraced by the fullness of grace. We know we are wisest when we are without words. When our tongues are paralyzed by awe, we recognize we are listening to the amazing grace of the Word of God. Let me share such a moment.

I got a call from my son. He had just been in a terrible accident, been ejected thirty-five feet in the air, only to land in a small mountain of snow left by the Highway Department near Albany, New York. His voice sounded feeble and fragile and soaked in hidden tears. I told him I was on my way. He sighed. I offered a million assurances, some verbal, some prayerful, many silent. I was so terrified. My fear bloated my soul to its breaking point. I could hardly contain the swelling anxiety within me. It was awful. It was like being infested by snakes.

On the drive there, I suddenly became calm. My son was alive. I was his father. I could not protect him from being sideswiped and ejected from his car. But I could protect him from a call to abandon all faith. I could be a living expression of faith. Not of the hokey or bumper sticker variety, but in offering the reassurance that he remained a beloved child of God, still here, still surrounded by a father and friends who adored him, and still capable of creating a good and wonder-filled future. I knew and he knew this would be incredibly difficult and there would indeed be significant post-traumatic stress. But I knew he would also experience faith stories which could create post-traumatic calm as well.

There is a still point in our souls. It is the calm center of the hellish hurricane of our lives. It is the lovely quiet which drowns out the din of our crazy culture, and all of it screams and shouts to pursue fame and fortune, and badgering us to death with the notion we are never enough. This still point is grace, and grace announces moment by moment that we are more than enough.

As I drove to see my son that day, I knew I was called to give voice to this quiet heavenly vision of a soul at rest. No, I am not speaking of rest as in "rest in peace." I am speaking of the rest which surpasses all human understanding and offers real rest for our weary souls. I had a whole heart of stories aimed at offering the healing balm of trust and calm and faith in a higher power. I would, and have been, a good storyteller for him.

Trusting Tears

"The soul would have no rainbow had the eyes no tears."
— John Vance Cheney

Faith stories often yield tears. It is one of the chief reasons we seldom tell them. We live in a culture which views tears as being a sign of fragility, weakness, or a lack of inner strength. But I believe tears are a sign of honesty and depth. Tears reveal compassion. Jesus wept at the loss of a friend. A weeping God is a good image for a God who fully understands our humanity.

Good stories produce tears because they speak of what matters. They pluck at our heartstrings by addressing our longings and yearnings and deepest desires. We are moved to tears by the Spirit of God. We are being moved to higher ground. We are being changed from hard-hearted to tender. Our kids need to be comfortable with their tears.

My late wife Patty was so incredibly comfortable with crying. Her tears flowed often and easily. At times I grew cynical, and I wondered if she chose to be a waterworks. After she died, I missed her tears. I realized how Patty had a great spiritual skill—empathy. She truly did feel the pain of others. I was amazed she could feel so deeply, but she could and she did. It was a gift. I know that now!

Patty's children were both adopted. No two children were more loved, however, than how Patty embraced each with her swollen devotion. Kristi, her daughter, long sought to find and know her birth mother. Patty helped Kristi find Linda. Patty was thrilled for Kristi to embrace Linda. I will never forget the Christmas when Linda, the birth mother, came to surprise Kristi, and how these two moms savored the sweetness of the moment. I was never prouder of Patty than when I witnessed her capacity to step back and let Linda take center stage. Patty's simple but exquisite faith was obviously present in her willingness to be in the background that Christmas. Christmas is Kristi's birthday, and Patty's gift to her was to choose to celebrate the inclusion of Linda in our lives.

Our kids, especially our youth, need to learn compassion. It is strange to say this, but our kids need to know the wisdom of weeping. They need to be easily and frequent and deeply touched. They need to have hearts which are tender and bleed and ache. They need to be sensitive. They need to be empathetic. They need us to teach them how to forgive everyone for everything.

They need to witness in us a maturity in our loving and in our forgiving. True love and true mercy both demand tears…often. One cannot lie and cry at the same time, and so God has given us tears as the medium of truth-telling. This is why our stories are so often told with and to tears.

Following

Faith is all about following. But we live in a culture which abhors following. Faith is obedience. But our culture wants to declare a freedom void of obedience. Faith is walking down a road seldom traveled. But our culture chooses to drive down a freeway at dangerous speeds, taking the risk of being yet another fatality. Slow is not an option. Wandering is called being lost. Meandering is thought of as pointless.

Following is movement. It is growth. It is maturation. It is the process of becoming. Following is ironically becoming the best we can be, and arriving at a significant level of adulthood. When the culture says bigger is always better, our faith speaks of a spiritual longing for less. When the culture asks us to move at a furious pace, our faith asks us to go one step at a time, slowly and deliberately. As culture strives for the top, our faith is more comfortable on the ground.

Our kids struggle hard with the concept of following. It will seldom offer cultural accolades and affirmations. They have a real mistrust in being led by anyone, and this may be most true when it comes to a God they can neither touch nor know as real. Kids are prone to race on ahead. They want to get there, and get there fast, no matter where "there" is.

Our kids have been raised on a warped concept of progress and an even sicker understanding of adulthood. They are asked to believe in almost anything as progress as long as it is fashionable or financially lucrative. They are encouraged to think what we label "adults only" is what the culture deems to be adulthood.

In the minds of many modern youth, following is for losers. Following is for those who have no dreams or drive or determination. Following is what those without willpower do with their paltry existences.

Our youth group was scheduled to clean a Lutheran resale shop in the inner city on a Saturday morning. The high school, where most of our youth attended, announced plans for a ski trip that same Saturday, since there had been a major snowfall on Thursday. The bus to go skiing was leaving at seven o'clock in the morning. We were scheduled to be at the resale store from nine until one in the afternoon. I received many calls of cancellation, several from dramatically apologetic parents reminding me that I should know what it was like to be a teenager. I also wanted to tell them I knew what it meant to be a Christian, but I bit my tongue.

Right on time, three kids straggled into the parking lot and climbed into my waiting car. I thanked them profusely for coming. Two girls declared they could not ski, and Cal—the only boy—was quiet and growled under his breath. It was a sound filled with disappointment and disgust. He would later make it clear his father had made him do it.

After cleaning for almost five hours, owing to our labor shortage, I took our small band of weary youth out for lunch. It was indeed the least I could do, or so Cal let me know. Over lunch we started talking about the resale shop. All three kids were stunned by three facts. The volume of trade was high. The customers were almost all elderly and white. Almost every single person who visited the store thanked us for cleaning. It had been a most meaningful morning, an eye-opener for these wealthy white kids from Whitefish Bay.

Cal was the last to be dropped off. He turned to me and said, "Pastor Bill, I really am glad I came. It felt good to help those folks out. There will be at least a dozen more ski trips this winter. My father didn't actually make me come. He said I needed to follow my heart. I did, and I am glad I did."

Faith stories are almost always about following the heart. The heart is the seat of the soul. The heart is what pulses with the wishes of God. The heart is usually true to a higher power and obedient to the tough climb up to higher ground. I told Cal I was proud of him for coming, and I suspected Christ was pleased as well. He gave me a bit of a grimace. I told him, like it or not, I had meant it. Cal nodded and went inside. I knew Cal would remember the choice he made that day.

First Will and Testament

Faith is our first will and testament. It is not the distribution of wealth and goods at the end of our lives. It is the decision to give love and mercy *throughout* our lives. The day we choose to be a person of great love, even the love of an enemy, and great forgiveness, even to the point of forgiving seventy times seventy, we are living our faith. This is the walk of faith and not merely the talk.

Many of our stories depict times of faith being made real. Faith is all about what ultimately concerns us. When we bear witness to our faith happening right before our very eyes, we take note and record these events as stories. If we fail to do so, we are missing out on a remarkable opportunity to mature and offer others our insights and depth. If our kids have no good faith stories to tell, it will be as the result of having lived life on the surface, choosing not to make a difference, and refusing to make hope happen.

We owe it to our children to teach them about the importance of the genuine good life. We owe it to ourselves, God, life, humankind, and them to mentor them about how to actualize their faith. We must gather up stories of faith over a lifetime. These truth-filled tales will reveal to our kids the best of who they are, and how the Kingdom of God is built brick by brick, inch by inch, mercy by mercy. These are stories of folks being significant. They are not success stories, but rather anecdotes which reveal humanity's drive to make the world a better place and become the people we believe God created us to be.

My cousin Candy was heavily involved in drugs and alcohol. She was in her early twenties, and most of the time we had no idea of how she spent her days or where she stayed at night. On one such night, my mother walked from our home into Racine's inner city and brought Candy home to stay. I asked my mom how she knew where to go, and more importantly, what she was thinking in bringing Candy here. She told me she loved Candy, and it was the right thing to do. I was also told not to ask any more questions—mom was tired. She had walked over eight miles there and back. She had also been clearly terrified on her mission to fetch her niece.

Candy was arrested a few months later. My mother had gotten wind that Candy faced jail time. My mother went to Candy's court date. The judge, Jack, was an old friend of my mother's from Park High School. When he said he needed to give Candy jail time, my mother stood up, went forward, took Candy by the arm, and told Judge Jack that jail was out of the question. She stated emphatically that Candy would be coming home with her. Mom then walked out of the court with her niece in tow. Judge Jack told me later he had never been more stunned in all his years on the bench.

I again asked my mom what she was thinking. She again told me it was the right thing to do, and she said I could be of help by offering love to Candy whenever I could. I was in Seminary at this point, and what I experienced my mother doing and being made my studies seem, well, quite irrelevant. Indeed, deeds are far greater than creeds.

Our children and youth need to see, hear, and be deeply touched by the goodness of faith. They do not need to memorize verses or prayers or doctrines. They do not have to toe the party line of the denomination. They need to experience faith alive. This is what will teach and transform them. These are the stories we must share with them so they know there are adults who are following God, seeking to live in God's image, and striving to build God's Kingdom, bringing heaven to earth.

Story Starters

- What stories truly inspired the formation of your faith?
- What are your ultimate concerns?
- What story always moves you to tears? When was the last time you witnessed an event which moved you to tears?
- Which stories in your life have offered you wisdom you've sought to follow?
- What personal story do you hope becomes a part of your legacy, one which others will seek to emulate or follow?

Section Three

INTRODUCTION

A Good Story Challenges Us to Mature

"A child becomes an adult when he realizes
he has a right not only to be right but also to be wrong."
— Thomas Szazs, *The Second Sin*

"Maturity is reached the day we don't need
to be lied to about anything."
— Frank Yerby

"You grow up the day you have your first real laugh—at yourself."
— Ethel Barrymore

"We need stories in order to understand ourselves, for good or bad,
to be inspired or horrified, it's how we cope with being human and
how we decide what type of person we will become."
— Lily Graham, *The Cornish Escape*

Maturity is at the core of every good story. The migration of maturity is the instinctual path of a good story. Maturity and spirituality are literally one and the same. If we are maturing, we are also becoming deeper spiritually, and growing into the man or woman God created us to be. Maturity is the pulse of life.

Our children are becoming desperate for information about maturing. Unfortunately, what they are receiving are messages about how to stay young forever, live lives they know are trite, lacking in substance, and obsessed with success. Our kids long to be given insight on how to find meaning in their days, and what it will take to enjoy their lives and to live them fully.

What will help our children most in the art of maturing is to be challenged by the mystery of life, to become enchanted by its magic, and to learn how to make a memory or miracle or both. Maturity requires that we adults guide them into experiences which enable our kids to walk humbly with their God, and to acquire significant wisdom as they age.

Life is quite difficult. It is very demanding. It is a long hard climb. It must be lived with integrity, dignity, simplicity, and yes, above all else, maturity. Our kids need assistance on how to live and age gracefully. They must be taught the arts and disciplines of love, forgiveness, and the leading of a good life. Good stories can reveal hope, inspire faith, create the capacity for love, and enable us to muster the strength needed to make good choices and be good people.

What I find truly disturbing in modern culture is how we encourage our children to grow down rather than up. Our kids are being incessantly badgered to become predictable, and never rock the boat. They are being asked to become a know it all. They are being taught to avoid embracing mystery, entering the wilderness, or facing the dark times of life—both physically and spiritually.

"Whoever perceives that robots and artificial intelligence are merely here to serve humanity, think again. With virtual domestic assistants and driverless cars just the latest in a growing list of applications, it is we humans who risk becoming dumbed down and ultimately subservient to machines."

— Alex Morritt, *Impromptu Scribe*

The good life in America has little to do with goodness. This is a good life with no depth, service or sacrifice, risk taking, star following, Kingdom creating, and certainly does not reflect the image of God. This is a life of trivial pursuits, a wasting of time, talent, and spiritual gifts. It is all about erecting monuments to ourselves and building towers up to the gods of success and power. This is a good life which will never give birth to a good story.

Most of all, this modern-day version of the good life is *childish*: greedy, demanding, lacking in civility and sincerity, often mean-spirited, and incapable of genuine love or mercy. We are creating generations of spoiled brats, young adults with little vision for a safer, saner, simpler future. In a society which is all about staying young, having more and more, where enough is never enough, and winning must include many more losing, we have managed to build a hellish pace, lifestyle, and people.

The genuine good life is not for the select few. It is not easy, nor is it about offering comfort to the already way too comfortable. It is a lifestyle which requires ample discipline. It will require rigorous honesty, an open heart and mind and soul, and ask of us to make choices which serve others, make sacrifices that can hurt, and delay gratification until we can include more of our brothers and sisters. This is a good life which is all about moments of joy, sweet satisfaction, and transformation. This is the life chosen by the wisest of us.

Teaching our kids to become wise is an art in itself. It is also our responsibility. The three wise men of the Christian Christmas story are wondrous examples of what we might teach our kids.

The wise men paid attention to the skies. They looked up. They looked for God's signature written on the stars. They were followers. They took the risk of leaving the settled comforts of home. They withstood the ridicule of family and friends and society. They went forth into a black night, lit only by stars. They went out into the wilderness of the desert, not knowing where they would wind up, or if they would find what their soul yearned to find. They went on an adventure. They took a pilgrimage. They followed their hearts, and were led by their souls. They lived their longings.

They followed a lone star, one which was brighter than all others. They got lost along the way—many times. They grumbled and complained and blamed one another for not knowing the direction to take. They kept the faith. They kept moving forward. They trusted their heart's desire. Their hearts led the way. They knew down deep they were searching for a new home.

The three of them came bearing gifts. This meant they came in an attitude of gratitude. Their perspective was one of feeling blessed, and hoping to share their own blessings. They struggled on, even as winds and rains and sand wailed, even as people they met snickered and snidely pointed out the foolishness of their whims. They slogged on.

They came to a barn out back of an inn. It stunk and it was cold. Nobody was there except for a tiny family with a tiny baby. The baby was howling, and the mother looked exhausted, and the father bewildered. It was a scene of exhaustion, poverty, fear, and societal ridicule. The three astrologers from the East knelt down. They set before the tiny child their gifts of gold, frankincense, and myrrh. They believed.

They knelt. This is crucial to maturing, knowing when to offer honor and homage, knowing when to be awed. The three men were wise enough to kneel before a powerless babe who owned not one thing, a little child of no wealth or status or fame. These three chose to kneel in front of who they believed to be a living reflection of a living God. They were home. They sighed and smiled. They remained in silence. They heard the Word of God. They listened to the heartbeat of the child.

Can we offer our kids such guidance? Will we encourage them to follow their own stars, and go on wild adventures into the night? Will we respect their spiritual travels, and where and when they choose to kneel? More importantly, will we value if they choose to look in unexpected places, and to worship at the feet of powerless kings? Will we be their mentors in the art of maturing, or their masters in the mindless pursuit of money?

Admit it—this is one damn tough choice to make. One route is safe and popular, while the other road is risky and wrought with fear. Growing up or down, popularity or creativity, maturity or materialism, a good life without goodness or one which creates only the best, which one? The stories we tell our children will reveal our answers.

Good stories offer our children the powerful gift of memory. We must counsel our children and youth about why memories are not only to be valued, even prized, but experienced as living guides. We are all of us a composite of our memories. It is memory alone which keeps us from being truly alone. Our modern American society has what the current Pope called "spiritual Alzheimer's." We have created a culture void of memory, and seemingly unable to recall the good sacred stories of our lives.

We must offer our children the gift of our memories, as written and spoken in our sacred stories. We must encourage our kids to hear tales of how we have found worth in our lives, and those who have influenced us in positive and productive ways. We must enable our youth to find genuine heroes, the courage to create, the will to be fully human, and the belief they too have divine stories to tell with their lives. We are sanctioned by God to help them mature and become the spiritual co-creators they are meant to be.

Jesus left a simple legacy for his disciples. He basically told them what to do and be in remembrance of him. His legacy was built upon a firm foundation of memories. We too must leave our children a legacy, and we too must leave them memories captured by our stories. We must challenge them to gather their own stories. We must be good storytellers for our kids, and teach them well, the art of looking and listening and experiencing the wondrous stories of our lives.

"Writers remember everything...especially the hurts. Strip a writer to the buff, point to the scars, and he'll tell you the story of each small one. From the big ones you get novels. A little talent is a nice thing to have if you want to be a writer, but the only real requirement is the ability to remember the story of every scar. Art consists of the persistence of memory."
— Stephen King, *Misery*

Story Starters

- What stories have taught you the most about the meaning of maturation?
- Which story would you credit with having inspired you to mature?
- Review those stories which revealed the nature of the genuine good life to you?

CHAPTER ELEVEN

A Good Story Challenges Us to Be Wise

"No man was ever wise by chance."
— Seneca

"People far prefer happiness to wisdom,
but that is like wanting to be immortal without getting older."
— Sydney J. Harris

"It requires wisdom to understand wisdom;
the music is nothing if the audience is deaf."
— Walter Lippman, A Preface to Morals

Wisdom is not knowledge. Knowledge is never wisdom's opponent. Wisdom does not require education, but education certainly eases wisdom's attainment. Wisdom is receiving, letting life teach us a lesson. Wisdom does not guarantee a full life, but it does require being fully awake and aware.

Wisdom is an informed heart. It is a smart soul. Wisdom is humble, tender, and thrives on forgiveness—both the getting and the giving. Wisdom is when the ordinary becomes extraordinary, the human divine, and the love unconditional. Wisdom is the language of grace.

Wisdom is always on high alert. It anticipates, and is ready to stop, look, and listen at a moment's notice. It is on notice. It pays strict attention to life. When it comes to spotting God's signature, wisdom is like a spiritual vigilante. Wisdom is on the move, maturing and growing, on the way to higher ground, and walking the walk.

Wisdom weeps. It is kind, sensitive, considerate, empathetic, and filled with compassion. A wise soul bleeds. It suffers with folks, binds wounds, and dries tears. Wisdom is fueled by tender mercy. It is fearless in face of human suffering and pain. Wisdom is possessed of the courage to confront evil. Wisdom wages war on bad news.

Wisdom walks humbly with God. It can both follow and lead. It carries crosses. It lifts up the burden of others. It is a team player. Wisdom chases beauty, stops for truth, and reveres life. Wisdom is often called to serve and sacrifice. Wisdom is frequently challenged with the task of building the Kingdom of God in the here and now.

Every good story contains a nugget of wisdom—often more than one. It is wisdom which makes the story a good one. It is wisdom which asks for the story to be told, and which inspires a storyteller to pass on a truth. The wise listen to and for stories. The fool has grown deaf to the sacred nature of stories.

I suspect our youth need and desire to be wise, in spite of being often overwhelmed by technology. Our youth long to be able to speak the truth, and yearn to be understood—which is to be truly heard. Our youth must become wise, however, and this is a journey of the soul, a pilgrimage which requires their full presence.

The Wisdom Way

"Everybody is a story. When I was a child, people sat around
kitchen tables and told their stories. We don't do that so much
anymore. Sitting around the table telling stories is not just a
way of passing time. It is the way the wisdom gets passed along.
The stuff that helps us to live a life worth remembering."
— Rachel Naomi Remen

We all possess wisdom. We all have been possessed by wisdom.
Wisdom is our nature, our calling, and our soul's delight. Wisdom is a
homing instinct we were blessed with at birth. Just as birds know when
to migrate, we too know when it is time to come home to God.

The wisdom way may be a long hard walk, filled with detours,
obstacles, and getting hopelessly lost—but, eventually we do arrive home
with God. Like the yellow brick road, wisdom will ultimately lead us
home. This is not a stroll but a determined sojourn. This is not a casual
walk, but a walk which takes us deep inside our hearts, minds, lives,
world, and God.

The wisdom way is primarily taught by stories. Good stories do not
offer maps, but they do point the way. Good stories offer no guarantees
we will not get lost, but they do offer the assurance we are headed in the
right direction. Wisdom has more than a few folks who are possessed of

a good sense of direction, and we would be wise to seek them out as our spiritual guides.

I gathered my youth group for a discussion with several select senior citizens, and asked them to please listen up, as they were about to hear some good stories. I had asked these elderly folks to speak to the youth about what they found truly mattered in their life journeys. I could sense that some of the youth were planning a sneaky exit, and I gave them a look which told them I would rearrange their faces if they did. They all stayed. Wise!

These wise older men and women, many of whom were well known in the community, quietly and slowly shared a few sacred tidbits of wisdom, and several wonderful and enchanting stories. Many of their stories also yielded tales of great tragedy, in three cases, the loss of a child—in birth, in a car accident, and by suicide. Many of their anecdotes were about the nature of Nature to teach us at all times, and how holy is God's good earth. A few spoke of their passionate love for a grandparent, parent, spouse, friend, memorable stranger, or God.

Everyone seemed to call upon examples of compassion and passion as their main source of wisdom. Whenever they were moved to tears by others or life itself, they had been graced by the hand of God. Whenever they had opened their hearts, offered a helping hand, or reached after life's true goodness, they felt themselves becoming wiser.

A few spoke of forgiving everyone everything. They all addressed loving unconditionally and with fierce determination and steadfast patience. Every last one of these seniors laid claim to the wisdom of how wonderful life could be and was when approached with deep gratitude.

My seniors got a standing ovation, which moved many to tears, and a few to extoll the good audience they had had, and how much it was appreciated. The youth left and may have quickly forgotten much of the amazing stuff shared, but—over the course of the year, I heard many of those pearls of wisdom which had been cast before them, being lifted up again by these young folks, and they still shined and gave life a lovely luster.

It is crucial to have our young people mentored by the wise, by folks who have walked the walk. Our youth are fantastic at knowing when they are hearing BS or truth. They have great God-given insight. They can hear it when someone is boasting, or humbly offering a lesson learned in life. Our youth are not solely impressed with the achievements of celebrities, no matter how hard our culture strives to make them so, and they do possess a spiritually urge, a yearning, a wanting to know how to enrich and enjoy their lives.

I was recently asked what I felt was most effective in addressing the massive issue of chemical dependency. I knew immediately. I offered how on three occasions on Shelter Island, a local AA group chose to break anonymity and share a meeting with youth. Nothing planned or staged, but an actual meeting, allowing the youth the rare privilege of being there to listen.

The kids were always stunned. They came expecting something almost cultic. They were moved to simply hear a story shared, and support offered, and a rare level of genuine honesty flowing from adults who were claiming a disease and not a weakness. They were always caught off guard by the simplicity, the honesty, and the intimacy of the sharing. They always spoke of how powerful it was to realize that nobody starts out wanting to be a drunk or an addict.

"The saddest aspect of life right now is that science gathers knowledge faster than society gathers wisdom."
— Isaac Asimov, *Isaac Asimov's Book of Science and Nature Quotations*

The Paradox of Wisdom

"The curious paradox is that when I accept
myself just as I am, then I can change."
– Carl Rogers

Wisdom is rooted in paradox. Wisdom is colored gray, while our culture prefers black and white. Wisdom does not seek to offer answers, nor does it claim certainty. Our culture celebrates those who pontificate on every subject under the sun, even topics for which they have no insight, experience, education, or background. If they are loud and obnoxious and willing to say anything at any time, they can probably find a place on TV or the radio, or sadly, even within the print media.

Jesus taught in parables. Parables are little stories which pack a wallop— big meaning. These parables are always soaked in paradox. These parables are known for wisdom, as they point to the grey light of grace. These parables reveal that every day we are living we are also dying. They remind us that when we are serving others we are at our most powerful. They tell us the truth that we often need to get lost in order to find our true selves. They admonish us on the wisdom of being folks who understand the first will be last, how spiritual outcasts like the Samaritans are frequently our best teachers, how grace never makes common sense, for its sense is most uncommon, and how most miracles are the result of raw mercy.

Life is a fusion of opposites, as is faith. As a Christian, I worship a human God. I celebrate Good Friday and Easter. I claim to understand and believe that in my weakness God is glorified. I am taught that the world will hate me as they hated Jesus. They hated him for knocking all of the rungs out of the ladder of success and status. They hated him for loving "those people." They hated him for loving and forgiving without condition—our own culture is all about conditions!

Those who are wisest in the world, and who have the most to teach our youth, will have come to master three lessons—so my life has wisely taught me. First, it is the will of God for humans to be human, and we spend a lifetime trying to be anything else. Second, we are of very little significance in the scheme of things, except we are a beloved child of God. Lastly, we have a choice in life, and it is between fear, which expects the worst, and faith, which expects the best.

The Dalai Lama, when asked what surprised him most about humanity, answered, "Man. Because he sacrifices his health in order to make money. Then he sacrifices money to recuperate his health. And then he is so anxious about the future that he does not enjoy the present; the result being that he does not live in the present or the future: he lives as if he is never going to die, and then dies having never really lived."

Wisdom is Seldom Pretty or Nice

*I was sobbing. I was preparing to conduct my first wife's funeral. I had been
working on her eulogy when I had been left dumbstruck by a revelation. This
was an epiphany of a kind, and like so many, it was neither nice nor pretty. It
was wisdom which cut away at the phony and the superficial, and exposed a
glaring weakness in me and my ministry and within my marriage to Christine.*

*I had spent a bulk of my married life trying to smooth out Christine's
rough edges. I had worked tirelessly to make her easier to swallow, less difficult
to be around, more culturally appealing, and far less strident and difficult
and demanding.*

*Christine was a big woman, with a big voice, a big laugh, and a ferocious
will. I often teased her that when she walked into a room, it was as if she were
giving everyone "the bird." I frequently tried to play teacher and encouraged
her to play nice with the other children. She would look at me and smile, and
say, "That is* your *issue. Deal with it!"*

As I prepared her eulogy, I finally got it. The epiphany—it was indeed
my *issue. I was a minister who sought to keep people happy, to be admired
and even adored, and to be charismatic and quite popular. Christine was
blunt and honest and a breath of fresh air. I suddenly recognized I had tried
to remove her rough edges, when those who would be attending her funeral
cherished and adored those very same rough edges.*

*Christine was a victim of incest. She spoke about, it, wrote about it,
and let it become her identity. She also had an abortion in her late twenties,*

which she often stated was the direct result of believing her purpose in life to be sexual—a frequent spiritual result of incest, she contended.

Christine was an outspoken feminist, and she challenged a male-dominated clergy every chance she got. She also lambasted her church for their historic failure to ordain blacks, women, and most recently, gays and lesbians. She told them of her disappointment in how far behind the church always seemed to lag on moral or ethical issues, and was so seldom historically on the right side.

Christine spoke easily and often about sex and sexuality. She was at ease in claiming her emotions and devout in her beliefs. She was a bleeding-heart liberal, and her compassion was as wide as the sky.

Christine battled the addiction of overeating until the day she died, which followed a second gastric bypass surgery. She also let it be known that many incest victims do not wish to be sexually attractive, and how weight becomes for them a major means of protection.

Christine preached of a Jesus who was first and foremost about preaching good news to the poor. She was wild in her intense dislike of the self-righteous, or those who saw themselves as superior souls. She believed her Jesus would find a way to bring everyone home, and though heaven was full to the brim, hell was for her—empty!

You get the picture. This was one powerful but fragile woman of faith. She was not here to make people happy. She was here to make us think and feel and believe, and to be better people than we thought we could be. She spoke of a higher ground upon which she daily walked. She picked up her crosses and carried them for her entire adult life.

I gave a damn good eulogy at her funeral. Only because I chose to celebrate all of Christine's wondrous and sharp rough edges. I named and claimed how uncomfortable she made us, and because of her, how much we had all grown and matured. This was a life well lived, and she was a good and faithful servant.

Christine Beth Rannie Grimbol was and is the wisest person I have ever known, and who has ever known me—inside and out.

When Wisdom Wins

Our youth need to know that wisdom does win. It is not as often as we might hope, nor as widespread, but it does occur, and every single day. They must gain respect for the quietude of these celebrations of wisdom's victories. There is no loud boasting. There is no condemnation of the defeated, for there are no defeated. Wisdom can only win when we all win.

When I look into the eyes of our youth these days, I still bear witness to the blessed presence of goodness. There are tears down there, in their guts, pools of tears which can claim bright joy and gray sorrows. Our young have compassion stored, and passion in reserve. They are awaiting being uplifted or ignited, and they do so long to be inspired. We must become those who follow close behind, blowing tiny breezes to set their dreams aloft, and helping keep their bubbled hopes safe from the prick of a cynical needle.

It was August and still plenty hot at 3:00 a.m. My grandmother and I were sitting on the front porch, watching the remnants of a brief but raucous thunderstorm head out over Lake Michigan. The lake was notorious for sucking these storms up, like a kid with a straw and an ice cream soda. Grandma was relieved we had not traveled to Oz, and somewhat embarrassed for having yanked her grandson out of bed and onto the front porch to watch. Though she claimed to delight in thunderstorms, I was well aware of my own mother's terror of them, and knew it came from somewhere—somewhere was seated in the rocker at my side.

She noted the emergence of stars and a silver sliver of moon. She commented that the breezes were cooling ever so slightly, and didn't the sheets smell lovely in the wind. She was quick to explain that she let them hang outside overnight, as the day's air was too wet, and they would need a second drying in tomorrow's sun. She gave a small squeal when we simultaneously noticed the fireflies scooting and skipping all about the bushes by the porch. I asked if I could get one of her fruit jars and try to catch a few.

"Whatever for?" she asked.

"So I can take them inside and study them, and name them, and have them as a night light."

"I think they will be better left outside in the cover of night."

"But, Grandma, I might be the first and best firefly collector."

"That is what you have a memory for, Billy. To recall the beautiful things you get to see."

"Well, I would like to have some to keep."

"Well, when they are truly beautiful, you can't."

"Can't what?"

"They are uncatchable. Besides, what is the point of having heaven in a bottle?"

"I don't want heaven. I want fireflies."

"They are one and the same."

For most of my childhood, as well as during a swift remembrance in adolescence, and on the wings of aging as an adult, I have often had a vision of heaven as a field of swarming fireflies. It takes my breath away, which is I guess what heaven is meant to do, and holds me in its spell for a long lovely moment of wonder and awe.

I somehow knew that Grandma had shared wisdom with me that night in the aftermath of an August thunderstorm. She had pointed out to me the foolishness of trying to capture heaven in a bottle, and why fireflies will lose their magic and mystery when confined and stared at through glass. She had spoken to me of the miracle of my memory, and my calling to remembrance.

Life must be gathered up in memory. Memory honors living by capturing our experiences in stories, and those stories serve as the real scrapbooks of our lives. Even more than a photo album or yearbook, it is our stories which reveal the truth of what happened and how it felt. It is like a giant jigsaw puzzle, and every one of us has a border of stories we must assemble before we can try to connect and interlock all the remaining bits of wisdom.

Let it be said, however, before we even begin, that there will always be a missing piece, and that missing piece must be filled by God.

Story Starters

- Define wisdom.
- Who is the wisest person in your life at this point? How and why?
- How does wisdom make a difference in the quality of our lives?
- Share a piece of paradoxical wisdom you have learned.
- Has your family shared stories of wisdom with you? Can you name and claim one to share?

CHAPTER TWELVE

A Good Story Challenges Us to Embrace the Dark

"What I am afraid of is the first thing I was ever aware of
being afraid of and what I have told my daughter
countless times she need not fear: being alone in the dark.
It is a small prison of emotion from which there is no escape.
It is also, in its own way, a shattering revelation."
– S.C. Gwynne

George was my first ever babysitting job. My mother told me our neighbor had chosen me as a good role model for her young son. I was a sophomore jock at Horlick High School—obsessed with being popular. George was a notorious little geek, and I knew him only from the sight of his thick glasses and how he always carried a huge pile of books. Not under his arm like a boy, but under his chest like a girl. I told my mother I would do it once, mainly because I needed money for the weekend.

George met me at the door and promptly took me to his room, which was loaded with scientific stuff. There was a large telescope, and three microscopes of different sizes. There was a mobile of the planets, and a poster of the Milky Way. I must admit his dinosaur collection was impressive, and his twin lizards managed to give me the creeps.

I asked him if he collected baseball cards. He said no. I asked if he had a favorite Milwaukee Brave. He said no. I asked about a favorite Packer. Again negative. I asked about his favorite school subject. No surprise there, science. I asked about good buddies, and he said he had none, and that he hoped I would be his first. I thought there was not a chance in hell of that happening.

His mother left us a vast array of snacks, showed me where the TV was located, told me what George's bedtime should be, and gave me his nighttime medications to administer before bed. She then said there was one more thing. She told me that George had a slight fear of the dark, but that he would probably be fine with me there.

Slight fear. That would be like calling the Grand Canyon a slight crack in the earth's surface. George cried and wailed for an hour. I left him alone, per his mother's instructions, but finally surrendered and went in and sat on his bed.

"Jesus, George, you have enough night lights in here to land a plane. What is the problem?"

"I just don't like the dark."

"What don't you like about it?"

"It is dark!"

"Duh! Of course, it is dark, George. That is so we can get some rest. Even the Earth needs to rest."

"It does? Why?"

"It gets tired of us playing on it all day and messing things up." Even I knew how stupid this sounded, but hey, I was new at this and working without a script.

"And I don't like boogeymen!"

"Have you ever seen one?"

"Well, no, but I know they are out there."

"How do you know?"

"I just do."

"Then let's go for a walk around the block and see if we can find one, and introduce ourselves."

"They will eat us up."

"No, they won't. They think humans taste sour, like spoiled milk." I was getting better at this gig. "Come on. Let's go."

"In my pajamas?"

"Nobody will see. It's dark."

"I am afraid. Are you?"

I answered with a resounding no, but knew in my heart of hearts that I had long harbored a deep-seated fear of the dark. So off we went on a genuine adventure. I held George's hand, and we began to adjust to the darkness. George was soon struck by how well he could see, and though he was easily startled by the sounds of barking dogs, slamming doors, or the occasional loud voice, George definitely enjoyed being out at night.

"Pretty cool, huh?"

"Yeah, look at all the stars. And that is a gibbous moon."

George went on to tell me all kinds of interesting stuff about the solar system, and I must admit to being amazed at his knowledge and the passion with which he shared it. By the time we had walked the entire block, George was clearly getting tired, and let go with a huge yawn. He told me he was ready for bed. I led him inside, pulled back the sheets, and tucked him in.

"Did you see any boogeymen, George?"

"Nope, did you?"

"Not a one."

"Maybe they don't come to the north side."

"Could be!

Soon, George really did not need a babysitter, and his mother proudly told me he had limited his night lights to two. She thanked me profusely for freeing her from the fury of George's terror or of the dark. I accepted the praise, but knew down deep I was equally grateful to George for having helped me with my own fear of the dark.

Life is dark, at least half of the time. We all must learn to cope with darkness, and spiritually speaking, we need to be able to embrace it. Darkness is the doorway to maturing. Maturation requires us to face the darkness of grief, guilt, suffering, hurt, and disappointment, the joylessness of excessive routine, and the hopelessness of losing faith.

Darkness demands encounter. Darkness promises the wild adventure of being visited by our deepest wishes and wildest dreams. Darkness is where life's most mysterious questions arise, and the place where doubts can be readily admitted. Darkness is also where we can find a dwelling called Sabbath, a miracle of calm which restores our energy and spirit.

"The winter solstice has always been special to me as a barren darkness that gives birth to a verdant future beyond imagination, a time of pain and withdrawal that produces something joyfully inconceivable, like a monarch butterfly masterfully extracting itself from the confines of its cocoon, bursting forth into unexpected glory."
– Gary Zukav

Me and My Shadow

"I really believe that all of us have a lot of darkness in our souls.
Anger, rage, fear, sadness. I don't think that's only reserved for
people who have terrible upbringings. I think is really exists
and is part of the human condition. I think in the course of
your life you figure out ways to deal with that."
— Kevin Bacon

We all have a dark side, and it's often called our shadow. This side is inhabited by those attributes and qualities we often struggle to accept. These are the features of our selves we may find disturbing and secretly wish to eliminate or reject. These are the aspects of our lives and souls which we may even be unwilling to acknowledge. Be it conscious or unconscious, we think of our shadow as revealing what we would most like to be rid of.

Many good stories are about folks who find a way to embrace their dark side, and learn how to squeeze the positive out of it. These are stories about a personal characteristic, long thought to be a liability or weakness, which when seen in a new light, becomes a force of maturation, even a source of goodness. Good stories offer us a new perspective about the darkness. Only in horror stories is the dark meant to be frightening. Most good stories enable us to make the darkness visible.

A good example would be our emotions: hurt, anger, worry, jealousy, envy, fear, insecurity, disappointment, or sadness, to name a few. We live in a culture that tells us to have our emotions in check, to never let them see us sweat, and to hide our tears. We are incessantly reminded how being emotional is thought to make us weak, indecisive, and incapable of being a strong leader. Our efforts to eliminate or control our emotions are futile, owing, I believe, to God's wish for us to use them for the purposes of insight, depth, and spiritual sensitivity. Emotions are God's vocabulary.

Flaws, failings, and flops, nothing could be more human, and yet our culture admonishes us to keep them secret. Good stories reveal the wisdom in claiming our mistakes, errors in judgment, or faults of behavior. When we name it and claim it, we can change it. What lies hidden simply festers and spreads. The fact is that what we think is most personal, is also most general. We have all screwed up, and at times we have done so in a big way, but good stories capture how a mistake, even a big one, can serve to create a previously unseen depth of character.

Our culture sends the wrong message to our youth concerning the dark side of the soul. It encourages them to be like volcanos, repressing their humanity for the sake of image, only to erupt in ways that can be dangerous. We live in a culture of keeping score, winning and losing, getting even, and viciously climbing to the top. Our youth are asked to function like robots, not as human beings who are the beloved children of God.

Our young must face the darkness. We cannot protect them from life's pain, nor prevent them from being hurt or suffering as a whole. Every life will have its share of burdens, be tainted by grief and guilt, and get lost in a maze of fear and failings. Every heart will be broken. Every soul will be shattered. Every mind will be stretched to the point of breaking.

Every individual must mature, and this means to come to know the beauty and power and even joy of the dark. In this world of ours, navigating by starlight will be required, and we will be called upon to serve as one another's night light on a regular basis.

"People are like stained-glass windows. They sparkle and shine when the sun is out, but when the darkness sets in, their true beauty is revealed only if there is a light from within."
– Elisabeth Kubler-Ross

Shedding Some Light on the Subject

"There are two ways of spreading light:
to be the candle or the mirror that reflects it. "
– Edith Wharton

Walking in the dark begs for us to be awake, aware, and on high alert. Since there is so little light, we must make wise use of what we have. We must be focused. We must pay attention, and notice things that may cause us to stumble. Walking in the dark requires a deep trust in our capacity to find our way, a belief in our inner core and its spiritual sense of direction. The heart will find its way, even in the dark, and those who know the way by heart, who could walk it blindfolded, will become our true spiritual guides.

For our youth, we must be their mentors. We must be their guides for walking in the dark. We must help them memorize the way. We must point out the detours and the dangers and the dead ends. We must be their flashlight, their candle, or that which sheds some much-needed light on the subject. They do not need to be protected from the darkness, or kept away from it, but guided through it.

We must be straight with our youth. We must come clean. We must offer them the truth of our own lives. We know what yields real satisfaction. We understand what will create good lives for our kids and goodness for the world as well. We simply must cease to extoll selfishness and greed as worthy goals. We must enable our youth to know the equal value of every child, regardless of color or creed or sexual orientation. We must create genuine hope, and that can only be done by expecting our youth to be people of real significance.

Our youth must serve. They must sacrifice. They must suffer. They must make choices to own less. They must be humble. They must see that trickle-down economics is rife with evil, and has nothing to do with building God's Kingdom. Our youth need to hear stories about real adults who are doing and being real people, and seeking to create a safer, saner, and simpler world.

Our young must be taught that life is not all about them, and that what we champion must be good for everyone on the planet. We must become better teachers and tutors of our youth, and what we teach must have greater eternal integrity, as well as spiritual maturity.

We are presently a people who once again dwell in darkness. Maybe all people have dwelt in darkness. We are challenged as adults who care about their young, to light their fires, ignite their souls, and give spark to their faith. We must shed some light on the subjects that truly matter: the living, the loving, the forgiving, and the building of a peaceful Kingdom. Our stories can inspire. They can radiate a bright light.

Eclipse

"A glimpse is not a vision. But to a man on a mountain road
by night, a glimpse of the next three feet of road may
matter more than a vision of the horizon."
— C.S. Lewis

*9/11. An historic event in America—a terrorist attack levels twin towers
of wealth and power. Thousands of innocent lives are lost. Evil has come out of
the shadows and flown into the bright September sunlight over Manhattan.
It was an astonishing and truly tragic event in our short history as a nation.*

*I was in Manhattan for a doctor's appointmen, only weeks after the
attack. It was a spiritually startling experience. I am unsure I will ever be able
to explain or share it properly. It was an epiphany for me. It was saturated
with the presence of God, and yet, it left me dumbstruck. It defied human
language and still does. It was, like so many biblical or spiritual events or
experiences, beyond facts.*

*What I felt that day was how Manhattan was in a blackout. Not
literally, as it was yet another spectacular September day of glittering sunlight.
However, the spirit was thick and dark and deeply in mourning. This was a
Manhattan of lament. The whole city was grieving, and the atmosphere was
swarming with sadness. The eyes of people held no sparkle, no light at all, just
a wincing pain, a pain of having been made keenly aware of the darkness of
the world we occupy. The air was heavy with the weight of tears, and there*

was an odd eerie silence. No honking or yelling or even speaking. It was like walking into a tomb. It was like the darkened light of a full eclipse. As if all of life was in shadows. Nothing was bright or radiant, and hope seemed just a tiny morsel. Manhattan was hanging by a spiritual thread.

As I walked, I did notice something else, something inspiring. People were simply being kind to one another, gracious, nodding, patting hands and shoulders, allowing folks to get by, offering a helping hand. Little was spoken, but actions appeared to be tender. There was a deep and abiding sense of mercy about.

I was witness that day to the first buds of hope. Folks were plowing their way up through deep darkness, navigating their way through a dirt made fertile by the rottenness of a few. These were buds of civility, a decision that life must go on, and that we can at least be kind. The good people of Manhattan were responding to a terrorist attack, by calming one another with care, concern, and compassion.

I was so sad that day, and yet so glad. I was so uplifted by the goodness I witnessed. I recognized what an opportunity this was to bring out our literal best. This awesome tragedy could yield a profound shift in spirit. Manhattan was being transformed. It felt lighter because of the light emitting from the people of this city. They were each the proverbial candle and the gathering of light, not yet substantial, but it was significant.

Had we not spiritually stumbled off into the stupidity of another war, this could have been the occasion for America to become a gentler, more gracious and generous nation. We could have regained the role of being the spiritual leader of the world, rather than once again seen as the spoiled adolescent who wants it all now, and on his or her terms. It is a shame, a damn, sad shame.

Those who dwelt in pitch black darkness had seen a great light. It was amazing the blossoms it did produce, the good sweet fruit, and the revelation unveiled. May we be mature enough to learn, again from what might have been, how hope must be harvested when it is in season.

Fairy Tales Can Come True

Fairy tales are lovely little stories. They are spiritual in nature. We call them make believe, because they strive to *make us believe*. A fairy tale wishes to make us better, happier, healthier, more hope filled, and truer to being the people we were created to be.

Fairy tales are always filled with dark places and people. Enchanted forests, huge castles that have dark dreary dungeons, tornados and hurricanes and tsunamis, oceans too deep for light to penetrate, mazes and swamps and wilderness—fairy tales are staged in locations where the light is either minimal or excessive.

There are also witches and dragons and Captain Hook. There are always black souls with which to contend, and hard choices which must be made. These choices appear at first to be grueling and difficult, but are later revealed to be as obvious as the nose on our face.

Good stories often have the feel of a fairy tale. They, too, are meant to make us believe, to impart a message, teach a moral, or reveal a truth. Good stories seek to inspire and transform us. Good stories help us know that darkness, though never devoured, can be defeated, the fog will lift, the despair consumed by hope, the joy return, and God will be present.

Our youth need such stories. Tales of becoming at home in the dark, finding our way through a menacing forest, or being freed from the dungeons we choose to live in. Our youth need us to share with them how we have come to believe, have hope, and know joy. Our youth must hear stories which offer them the wisdom of wizards, who can point out the beauty and goodness of black and white Kansas.

> "An age is called Dark, not because the light fails to shine,
> but because people refuse to see it."
> — James Michener, *Space*

Let there be darkness! The darkness offers perspective for the light. It is the spiritual contrast which makes the light glow or gleam. It is the context which lifts up the light, and frees it to radiate.

There is much to be seen and learned in starlight. The moon may offer just enough light to reveal a great idea, love, or hope of forgiveness. The darkness is often home to all that is holy, our prayers, our deepest silent worship, our longings and our yearnings, the wild passionate desires of our hearts.

The darkness can spiritually offer us a most creative Sabbath experience. A time to rest and heal and wonder and reflect, a time of knowing full well we are not God, a time of accepting our humanness and both our insignificance, as well as our sacred status as children of God, beloved and cherished and adored.

In the beginning, there was a thick swirling darkness which covered the black boiling seas, and from that chaotic brew came a Creation of such grandeur it can still take our breath away. The same is true every day of our lives. Our creativity requires chaos to produce the goodness, beauty, peace, justice, and hope we week. This dark chaos is the fertile soil for the magnificent blossoms of faith. These sacred stories, these spiritual seeds, must be planted deep within our children.

"In the light, we read the inventions of others;
in the darkness we invent our own stories."
— Alberto Manguel, The Library at Night

———————————

Story Starters

- Were you ever afraid of the dark? How did you conquer your fear?
- What would we find, were we to explore your dark side?
- What does it mean to you to embrace the darkness?
- When was your life at a point that could legitimately be called one of your darkest hours—an eclipse?
- Is America a land which dwells in darkness? How and why? What would it mean for Americans to truly see a great light?

———————————

CHAPTER THIRTEEN

A Good Story Challenges Us to Embrace the Wild

"If you look throughout human history...the central epiphany of
every religious tradition always occurs in the wilderness."
– John F. Kennedy

"Civilization no longer needs to open up wilderness; it needs
wilderness to open up the still largely unexplored mind."
– David Rains Wallace, *The Dark Range*

*We had a new family in the neighborhood. She was divorced with two
children. She had sizable breasts and wore short shorts in the summer. To the
doughy women of my front porch, who gathered nightly for conversation and
juicy bits of gossip, she was scandalous.*

*I often lay in bed at night and listen to the porch ladies dissect the
neighborhood and ruminate on the worsening world. This particular night
they were scrutinizing Nancy, the new divorcee, and what they referred to as
her wild children.*

*I knew both Ed and Richie, and they were nice boys. I kept trying to
think what was meant by wild. All I could come up with was that they both
knew how to hunt and fish and climb trees, and they also claimed to know*

how to take apart a go-kart engine, and put it back together. They did cuss now and then and did so even in front of their mother. Ed, the oldest, talked about sex and boobs and butts, while Richie just nodded and smiled. But most boys my age did one of the two.

I finally asked my mom why they called Ed and Richie wild. She grimaced and stated that it was obvious. These two boys were left alone on a regular basis. Ed was in charge of Richie after school until Nancy got home at supper time after work at Hamilton Beach. Ed was also allowed to watch Richie on Saturday night, when Nancy went to Douglas Bowl for three games and three beers.

"Why is that wild?" I innocently asked.

"Well, they are children, and to be left to their own devices is highly inappropriate."

I had no idea what a device was, but I figured out that wild had something to do with being out of their mother's control. It had to do with being on your own, and free to do whatever you pleased. I had never been jealous of Ed and Richie before, but I sure was now.

"Why is that so bad?" I again asked.

"Well, because it is the first step to becoming a hooligan and running wild in the streets."

I, for the life of me, could not make the connection. How Ed watching out for his younger brother would be the first step to running wild in the streets, and how that would be the eventual pathway to Waupun, where our state prison was located. This was the logic of mothers and to the summer evening gatherings of the worry warts.

All I knew was that I longed to be Ed and Richie, and thought of being wild as something exotic and different, and exciting as all hell. My fantasies of being wild were extravagant and soaked in a deep seeded secret yearning to feel free.

We live within a culture of control. Americans are taught to play it safe, choose security over just about anything, and make sure we are in charge of our own fate. We are a people who *are* encouraged to stay in the lines and not risk stepping outside the box. We are a coloring book culture, and we never question who drew the lines in the first place.

Most parents think of themselves as akin to "bowling bumpers." Parents do not want their children to experience the humiliation of the gutter. Parents strive to make sure the spinning ball does not veer off course into the gutter. Parents also want that strike. They will jump up and down for a strike, even if it hit the bumpers three times going down the lane.

When I was ten, I received several paint-by-number kits for Christmas. I enjoyed art, and my folks thought this to be an ideal gift. By the end of the holiday vacation, I had completed every one of these so-called paintings. My mother asked me why they were not adorning my bedroom walls. I told her it was because they were not mine—really. She argued for a short bit, but surrendered to my disdain of only copying the work of those who chose the subject, divided the painting into small sections, and even selected he colors. I told her it would be a lie if I signed one of these pieces of art. She reluctantly nodded. I threw them all away by Easter.

The point of a paint-by-numbers kit was guaranteed success. This is also the goal of our culture, especially as it relates to youth. We are ceaselessly trying to make sure our young will be successful, have way more than enough, and be secure for the future. We want our youth to have happy, pain-free lives, with minimal worry, and maximum positive results. We want signs of wealth and achievement, and we wish to wear it as a designer tag on almost everything we own.

Our culture scoffs at those who choose the wilderness. They are the odd ducks who might even choose to reside in the wilderness, and spiritually speaking, follow the beat of a very different drum. Our youth are discouraged from taking any risk that might knock them down a rung on the ladder of success, or prevent them from attaining financial security—a level which, when achieved, will automatically rise. We train our youth to be people pleasers, performers, and perfectionists.

I was an in-control adolescent. I worked diligently and daily to keep everyone happy, to be popular, and to be part of the "in crowd." I was always juggling twenty social expectations in the air, and if one dropped, I would stay up nights worrying if someone witnessed my mishap. I despised being out of control, and seldom displayed my real self. I kept my feelings and true thoughts hidden, presented a carefree image, and acted as if I had the world by the tail. I was very popular, and my life seemed pretty damn perfect.

When the sixties hit, and I was in college at St. Olaf in Northfield, Minnesota, I suddenly explored being a rebel, but only when it was in fashion. My long hair, tie-dyed shirts, and frayed and holed jeans were not signs of a soul unleashed, but just cultural permission to look wild. The closest I came to actually being wild was marching in war protests. If the truth be told, I was so terrified of Vietnam, I was protesting out of pure fear, not any conviction or courage.

I am no longer shocked by the remarkable power of conformity. The need to belong, fit in, and gain the approval of those others, is enormous, and for many adolescents, obsessive. I have sadly born witness to several young people who wanted to write a great novel, sing or dance on Broadway, be an artist or poet, change the world, hike a wilderness trail, build a cabin in the woods, make a difference by serving others, be a prophetic voice for change, or follow their bliss, choose instead to be successful by cultural standards—success without much satisfaction.

The soul is wild. It was never meant to be controlled. God never intended for the soul to become predictable or the human spirit to be forced into rigid routine. The soul seeks out the wilderness. It goes there to be renewed and refreshed, and to feel at home again. The wilderness is the soul's true home. The wilderness, like the soul, must never be sold.

Stories speak to the soul. Stories target the soul, and aim directly for our heart of hearts. Good stories are often like a voice crying in the wilderness, calling us to a new way of living, challenging us to mature and grow and deepen, and encouraging us to be the poet, artist, mystic, rebel, and prophet we were created to be.

"If you read fairy tales carefully, you'll notice they are mostly about people who aren't heroes. They don't have special powers, or gifts. Often, they are despised as stupid. They are bullied, beaten up, robbed, starved, and they find they are stronger than their misfortunes."
– Amanda Craig, *In a Dark Wood*

The Wilderness

"In wilderness I sense the miracle of life,
and behind it our scientific accomplishments fade to trivia."
— Charles Lindbergh

The wilderness can be blindingly bright. So bright it can make us wince. So bright it creates a heat which could melt a star. In wilderness light we move slowly, as our spirits cannot ward off the intense heat and light of the desert. The soul must slither like a snake across the dunes. The soul does, however, possess a divine instinct for where the oases can be found.

The wilderness is like a vast ocean, at times as placid and peaceful as unwrinkled silk, then in a moment, wild with fury which may swell to mammoth dimensions. The wilderness takes us on a journey. It is like a raft weaving its way down the rapids of a river. There is no true guiding of the craft, simply offering the vessel the occasional "suggestions" of the oar. The wilderness is like the universe, vast and magnificent, and always on the move—always leaving. The wilderness is a solid metaphor for the spiritual act of maturing.

"We must go beyond textbooks, go out into the bypaths and untrodden depths of the wilderness and travel and explore and tell the world the glories of our journey."
— John Hope Franklin

The wilderness is seldom popular. It remains remote and populated by few. The wilderness is never in fashion, only sought by those who feel spiritually connected. The wilderness is wild at heart, raw and real, the essence and soul of nature, the core of Creation. At first glance, the wilderness appears to be empty, but is in fact teeming with life. The wilderness has a voice, but it is the silence which speaks, and tells wondrous stories of God's dreams for our lives.

The wilderness is never greedy. It has nothing to sell. It has no products to market. There is only the experience, and it is free. The only profits registered are in gratitude and serenity. The soul feels safe there—remember that.

Jesus sought the wilderness when he needed to reconnect with God. He went there to pray, meditate, and spiritually be nourished by the speaking silence. He went to the wilderness to hear his soul, a soul which told him stories. These wilderness stories, would point the way to the Kingdom of God, where humanity might even do things far greater than Him.

The wilderness can be a patch, a spot, wide as the sky, or deep as the sea. There is wilderness everywhere. We must stop and look and listen and be in touch with our own souls, as only then will we tingle with the transforming presence of the wilderness. There can be a wilderness in a child discovering a sea shell, or an adult meeting death face to face.

The Rebel

"Who am I? I am the spine that mountains hang upon!
I am the tears that the rivers cry! I am the lungs
that breathe the wind! I am the wolf that kills the stag,
the hawk that kills the mouse, the spider that kills the fly!
I am the stag, the mouse and the fly that are eaten!
I am the snake of the world devouring its tail.
I am everything untamed and untamable!"
— Patrick Ness

Young people are meant to rebel. They are created by God to challenge the adult world to change and grow and mature, just as they themselves must do. Adolescence is a time of rampant passion, innocent arrogance, and unbridled hope. A teenager who fails to rebel will be haunted by that a missing piece for the rest of his or her life. The teen that only keeps adults happy, often living out his or her parents' dreams, will eventually feel a deep anguish of the soul. Rebellion is our truest means of becoming our own true human selves.

We must encourage our young to be rebels with a cause. We need to raise young adults who will fight for their dreams, and seek to actualize their vision for the world. They must be angry voices at times. They must upset the status quo, and they must offend those who believe they alone know what is right. As adults and parents, we are called to help our kids become confident and convictional adults. We must enable them to navigate their way through a treacherous passageway called adolescence.

Good stories often tell the tale of rebels, those folks who dream big, risk often, and follow their hearts. These sacred stories speak of folks who are not necessarily popular, and who seldom if ever conform to the crowd. They fly solo, and are unafraid to chart a new course across the sky. They take a leap of faith. Most all good stories take such a leap. They record the flight of the soul. They tell us of our wings, and our capacity to soar.

> "I like a little rebellion now and then.
> It is like a storm in the atmosphere."
> — Thomas Jefferson

The Poet

"Poetry is an echo, asking a shadow to dance."
— Carl Sandburg

This is quite embarrassing, but I am not at all ashamed of it. When I was a junior at St. Olaf, I decided I would be a poet. I bought a beret. Yes, that is the embarrassing part, and I even had a vest I wore only when I wrote—even more embarrassing, and quite the ugly garment. I had a sacred place, a small island in the middle of a pond on the campus of Carleton College. I would walk the mile and a half to my spot, adorned with beret and vest, clutching a leather journal I had purchased. I would then play poet, drink wine, and write the afternoon away. I did this on several autumn and spring days.

What I wrote was not truly poetry, although it did attempt to be concise in its diction, and holy with its subject matter. I would only write about life's biggest questions or seek to capture snippets of beauty or ugliness, or desperately try to make a profound statement of some kind—usually political. I did not labor much over my words, but trusted I had something of significant worth to say, and so, I just let it flow. The feeling I got playing poet was excellent. It was the perfect fusion of calm and exhilaration.

I recently reread the journal. I can confidently say I was not much of a poet. However, there were lines which were insightful, powerful, foreshadowing, deeply spiritual, and which openly sought God. The enterprise was neither silly nor a waste of time. It was good to play with words, and explore the caves and caverns of life's great truths. It was a splendid thing to wear a beret and try to be someone who had something to say about life as a whole. On a few occasions—very few—I did have something to say.

I no longer have the beret or the vest, but I have chosen to keep the journal. I still write poetry of a kind, usually long prayers which strive to expose my soul. I am not sure if the seeds for such prayers were planted forty plus years ago at St. Olaf, but I suspect so. This I know for sure—all poets believe they are in contact and communication with the Spirit.

I played at poetry once, and somehow came to believe I could be a poet. It was a true leap of faith, and I still take one now and then. I believe we all are poets of a kind. At least we all bleed like poets, occasionally wearing our hearts on our sleeves, and just about everywhere else for that matter. Poets are bleeding hearts, as is the human race, if we are being true to the way and why we were created.

Poetry is carefully chosen words. Some may rhyme, most do not. They have harmony and a cadence, a rhythm. They sprout with visions and voices. They paint a picture. They tell a story. A good poem seeks to craft a message in images, enabling us to experience the holiness in a moment. All poetry is a valiant attempt to touch the sky, grasp a star, or be held by God; some succeed smashingly, and some fall flat. Each wishes to be a revelation—an epiphany of a kind.

Playing poet is good for the soul. It builds spiritual stamina, and releases the toxins of stress. The goal of poetry is not publication, though this may be a dream fulfilled by some, but is a burning desire to express something of ultimate concern. It is the venting of a passion. It is the soul grasping water.

Our kids need to see themselves as poets, and to understand poetry as a worthy activity. They need to see poetry as Sabbath, as a way and means to center the soul, in order to become people who can make a difference. Poetry offers up our vision of the difference we hope to make, and gives voice to our yearning to transform and be transformed. Those who opt to be poets should be celebrated as souls who found a way to higher ground.

The Artist

"All children are artists.
The problem is how to remain an artist once he grows up."
— Pablo Picasso

Life is an art. It is a demanding discipline. It is an act of creation. We are its artists, and we are each provided a wide spectrum of brushes, papers, and boards, and an amazingly diverse number of color palettes. When we see ourselves as artists in life and living, we lay claim to having a choice. We declare our stories to matter, and make a commitment to put them on paper or canvas. As artists we will not wait for life to create us, but actively engage life and its Creator in the artistry of being alive.

Good stories speak of spiritual artists, individuals who have created lives of meaning and value. Good stories speak to us of how some folks manage to paint a life in bold and brilliant colors; a mood in the somber tones of the earth; or an identity in black and white, and a vast array of grays. Good stories are told in all colors, and may be a portrait, a landscape, a still life, or an abstract. Good stories reveal a wide range of styles, from photo realism to Monet impressions, from the classical use of light in Rembrandt, to the wild swirling objects of Van Gogh. There is never one style alone which can tell a good story.

When our kids think of themselves as artists, they somehow not only mature, but become kinder and gentler people. The role of the artist is to capture beauty, or to reveal truth. As an artist, our young will behave as if their thoughts and actions and beliefs not only matter, but have real consequences. This will encourage our young to make thoughtful, even prayerful, decisions and choices, and to consider the impact of what they choose to create. If we don't care about what we create, we will never seek to reveal God in it.

Artists are not necessarily artsy-crafty. Being an artist is an attitude, and a perspective. The artist declares life to be worth watching. The artist points and says, "Don't miss that!" The artist stands on his or her head, legs and feet wildly kicking, and tries to get us to pay attention. It is the function of the artist not only to notice, but to recall, remember, even recapture that which dazzles with beauty, or creates waves of awe, or send a shiver up and down the spine.

The Prophet

"The task of prophetic ministry is to nurture, nourish, and evoke
a consciousness and perception alternative to the consciousness
and perception of the dominant culture around us."
– Walter Brueggemann, *The Prophetic Imagination*

Prophets are messengers. Prophets deliver notes from God. Prophets poke and prod and push. A prophet will often choose to be dramatic, offensive, arrogant, rude, tenacious, fierce—*wild*.

Prophets have a point to make, and they believe it to be urgent. Biblical prophets felt they were called by God. Some contemporary prophets do as well, but most simply feel compelled or driven to do so. They believe they have something they must express, or the world desperately needs to hear.

I have had the good fortune of coordinating at least a hundred different youth services. I would venture a guess, that half of those services featured a youth sermon which was truly prophetic. I have listened to youth challenge adults to be more protective of the earth, less racist or sexist or homophobic, and to admonish their church family to claim their own greed or disregard of the poor. I was always proud of how these young people captured the spirit of Christ's ministry; frequently oblivious of having done so.

Our youth must learn the vital spiritual importance of prophets. They need to know how badly our culture must be challenged to clean up its act, or to lift itself up to higher ground, or even return to some of the basics of their faith—like service and sacrifice. Our youth have few adult prophetic role models these days, and from a faith perspective, might have trouble naming one. This is a sad statement on the spiritual state of American culture—the absence of prophets.

I have had the good luck of spending time with Archbishop Desmond Tutu. The Archbishop comes to Shelter Island for rest and relaxation, and to spend time with our mutual writing agent, and beloved friend, Lynn Franklin. Whenever I have been in his company, I have been struck by two things. First, he is so full of joy. He just seems to love his life, and it oozes from every pore. Second, he cannot stop being a prophet.

Tutu just keeps opening his heart and his mind and his mouth, and he cannot keep himself from creating controversy. I just completed reading a recent book of his, *God is Not a Christian*, a wildly provocative collection of essays and speeches and sermons. Suffice it to say, the title alone is a proud proclamation of being a prophetic voice.

We too, and especially our youth, are being called in these modern times, to create with wild raw energy, and to become forces for peace and justice and the celebration of true equality. We are being challenged daily to save our good earth, and to become a good people living out the genuine good life. We are *all* being challenged to be prophets.

When something grows wild, it often does so in abundance—so it is with the soul. The soul is always wild. The soul thrives best when it is out of control—called surrender. When we "let go and let God," we are finally free to be the creatures God created us to be. When the soul is being true to its wild calling, being a rebel, a poet, an artist, and a prophet, the soul will be ready to turn the world upside down—which is exactly what God would hope and ask.

Justin called me with the wonderful news of his wedding plans. The wedding had been moved. He was getting married in Fort Davis, Texas. I had never heard of Fort Davis, Texas, so I asked him to please repeat the news. He told me how he and Heather had stayed there for a few days, and fell in love with the owners of a small inn. He also extolled the stunning beauty of the town and the surrounding mountains. I told him I would be there. When I got off the phone, I cussed him out for an hour. Having to travel to Texas in the middle of March? What are you, nuts? Plus, the thought of me in a cowboy hat was appalling, and I hoped it involved no horseback riding.

Later, he would explain to me they had decided to avoid all the hassles of trying to hold a big fancy wedding in Maine, which is where Heather was from, and where the guest list would have been way too long making things way too expensive. Fort Davis meant a casual and intimate affair and was right up their alley. Still, it was a shock and a trek.

When he told me the wedding reception would be at the local drug store, I nearly passed out. Even when he bragged about the menu—steak and baked potatoes and grilled asparagus, and a homemade sheet cake—I felt a deep longing for a normal child.

Then I remembered. His late mother, who sadly would not get to see this event, but had raised him to take risks, step way outside of the box, and to be true to his own heart, plus, as he mentioned to me on several occasions, his mom would have wanted him to make Heather happy, and he was doing just that. This was mostly her dream.

To say the least, the whole wedding was wonderful—every single moment. Our visit to the Rattlesnake museum, star gazing at a nearby observatory, brisket burritos at an outdoor restaurant, several planned hikes, and, of course, the reception at the Drug Store. The meal was scrumptious, and we were treated like royalty. It seemed as if all of Fort Davis saw themselves as the hosts of this wedding.

As for the wedding, well, the church was tiny and all wood, and made you think of Little House on the Prairie, *and everywhere there were all kinds of wild flowers in cobalt blue vases everywhere. Their vows were sweet and simple and from the soul. The readings shared were deep and funny and felt holy. It was truly just perfect.*

Justin and Heather have chosen a life in rural Vermont which follows a road less traveled. They are true to themselves and a calling to a saner and simpler existence. Justin's mother would be so pleased to know that she succeeded in raising a son who is true to his soul—and his wife. I suspect she does know.

Our kids deserve parenting which is not the equivalent of cloning. Our youth do not need protection as much as they need to trust in a Higher Power. We need to believe in God, and allow God to lead, no matter how we understand or relate to that God. Good parenting is not about teaching our youth to play it safe. It is about tutoring them in the art of being human and fully alive. What we owe our young is not to advocate the sale of the soul, but to enable them to know how to nourish that soul.

Good stories are a prime means of spiritual nourishment. Good stories insist on being true to our inner core, and to living out our unique personal truth. Good stories never lift up the predictable, or encourage mindless repetition, but invite us to know the myriad wild possibilities of being alive. Good stories are usually wild and rambunctious, and celebrate the unexpected and even shocking, even a wedding reception at the local drug store.

Story Starters

- When was the last time you chose to step outside the box? Why?
- How do you choose to celebrate diversity? How does your family?
- What is the spiritual role of the wilderness in your life? Are you a rebel? A poet? An artist? A prophet?
- When have you made a truly wild choice, and how did you fare?
- Why does the soul seldom play it safe?

CHAPTER FOURTEEN

A Good Story Challenges Us to Embrace the Mystery

"I would rather live in a world where my life is surrounded by mystery than live in a world so small that my mind could comprehend it."
— Harry Emerson Fosdick

Look through a telescope or a microscope. Look deeply into a child's eyes. Behold the seasons. Contemplate the complexity of the human brain, or marvel at the myriad functions of the human body.

Fully experience the death of a loved one. Make love with your eyes wide open. Look out over the sea. Look into a human soul. Look at the impact of a single life. Listen to a belly laugh, or the wind whispering, or the sighs of folks being reunited.

Our lives and our world are loaded with beauty and goodness and yes, with abundant mystery. Life is literally swarming with mystery. Sadly, we have become so callus and rigid and patterned in our living, we often fail to embrace this mystery. We simply fail to stop...look...listen.

We don't notice. We are not paying attention. We are fixated on what we know. What we can control. What makes us feel certain, the wonders of our own mind, and the knowledge it contains. Still, the mystery is all about us, seeking entry, poking and prodding us loose, trying to get us to come back to life—only this time on God's terms.

I was seven, and my dad had named me his co-pilot for our trip to Elmira, New York. Elmira was where he had gone to learn how to fix electric typewriters for Remington Rand, and his landlady while there had invited him to bring his family back for a vacation. I suspect she was stunned when he chose to accept the invitation. We were on our way.

About two hours from home, we entered the maze of highways which went in and out of downtown Chicago. My father assured us he knew exactly where he was going. My mother started to sigh and mumble under her breath. I noticed that Mayor Daley had welcomed us to Chicago for the fourth time—at least according to the neon green and white signs. By the time Mayor Daley welcomed us for the seventh time, I decided to mention it to my father.

My father proceeded to tell me he had been driving for twenty-five years, and that this was his old stomping grounds, and he knew the way. My mother blurted, "No, you don't Lenny, so get off the freeway, find a gas station, and ask for directions." He assured her he would not need to do so.

About an hour later we finally pulled into a gas station, and my mother was sent in to ask for directions. She returned to the car and told my father he was heading toward St. Louis and not the Indiana Turnpike. Then she screamed, "Why can't you just admit when you are lost?" My dad was silent.

Until the day he died, I don't ever recall him admitting to me that he did not know the answer.

Mystery demands that we surrender. Mystery begs us to wave the white flag. It pleads with us to accept that we just do not know, not the way, not the answer, not the reason, not the point or purpose, and not the heart or mind of God. We are lost.

Mystery confronts us with the truth that we haven't got a clue. The paradox is that mystery, once embraced, begins to create in us the capacity to understand. Mystery, like the kind gas station attendant, will offer us directions to get back on track.

Every good question is grounded in mystery. Each time we are left dumbstruck or blown away, we are held in the arms of mystery. Every good mystery teaches us that though we think we have all the answers, we know the way, we don't, and then it goes on to tease us with the possibility we just might have a clue as to the answer.

All good mysteries offer brief glimpses of answers, answers which evaporate quickly like a morning dew, or as fast as the drop of closely watched sunset. Mystery simply creates more mystery. Like the universe, the greatest mystery of all, it just keeps on expanding.

As we age, without question, the body does begin to shrink. The soul, on the other hand, begins to expand, to stretch in all directions, to reach for the stars, and seeks to grasp the hand of God. It is our human nature, our spiritual journey, to experience a soul restless to return to its Maker. Our spirit is designed reach out to the mystery, not so much for answers, but for clues and hints and insights as to what matters in Life.

We owe it to our children to prepare them for this spiritual journey. We need to equip them for such growth, and to warn them of the tragedy in selling or shrinking the soul. Our kids need to understand that we have a choice in maturation, and to be unafraid of aging or dying. We need to help our youth see their lives wondrous, an opportunity to be fully alive, awake, aware, and ready to make healthy choices. Our youth must not be trained to be a know it all, or to believe in their own grandiosity, but to celebrate being a human being.

So many of our young are consumed in creating an image, but sadly, it is not the image of God they choose to reflect. Technology, the domain of the illusion of certainty, has swamped our teens with the belief they can be in complete control of their lives and their world. It is a horrid set-up for addiction, depression, suicide, and most of all, the sale of the soul to the highest bidder.

We can take hold of our children's hand, and invite them to take a leap with us, a leap of faith, a leap out into the waiting arms of life's many and magnificent mysteries. What wonders we will then behold. Wonders technology cannot even touch, like beauty, goodness, mercy, joy, and yes, love.

A Revelation

"Cease trying to work everything out with your minds.
It will get you nowhere. Live by intuition and inspiration
and let your whole life be Revelation."
— Eileen Caddy

Her hair was actually blue, like the water surrounding an iceberg. She had to be well into her eighties, maybe even nineties. She was draped in an afghan in spite of the stifling heat outside, and the minimal air conditioning in the restaurant. She was being pushed in a wheelchair by a wincing man who I assumed was her son, and a grimacing adolescent who was definitely her granddaughter.

I was seated in a booth, having inhaled a doughboy burger with fries, and apple pie ala mode. I felt lousy, not only about what I had just eaten, but the state of my ministry at the time. I had just finished preaching, and had received nary a single positive comment. I was deep in the hole of questioning my calling. The arrival of this trio served as a visual aid for my spiritual condition. Could life possibly sink any lower than an old lady in a wheelchair accompanied by her bored-out-of-their-minds son and granddaughter?

The lady of the blue air did not even look at the menu, but ordered exactly what I had had, with the inclusion of a vanilla shake. Her son sought to have her order something more substantial, and went through all the entrees on the left side of the menu. She smiled and nodded and told the waitress she was having the Doughboy Special. Her son ordered the pot roast dinner in some kind of retaliation. The rail thin granddaughter ordered a salad with the no-fat dressing on the side.

I found the whole scene depressing, especially noting that the threesome never spoke to one another other than the son's efforts to cajole his mother into a different menu choice. I stood to leave and tried not to stare at the three silent miserable souls at the booth opposite me. As I walked past them, the lady of the blue hair gently grabbed my hand. I was still wearing my clergy collar, and so she called me "Father." I wisely decided not to try to explain I was Protestant. I mean really, who cares!?

"Father, this is my beloved son Arthur, and his beautiful daughter, my granddaughter Meredith. We are just having a lovely day. We went for a ride along the lake front, and now I am having the doughboy burger and fries, and apple pie ala mode for dessert. I even got myself a vanilla shake. I just love to have some sugar and grease when I get sprung from the home. I mean, how many nights can you eat tapioca and mashed potatoes—which taste exactly the same? Make sure you stop and see the lake when you leave. It looks like aqua marine corduroy. Just stunning! We take that lake way too for granted. You have a wonderful day, Father. God manages to bless us each and every day, now doesn't He?"

I gave her a little peck on the cheek and thanked her son and granddaughter for showing the lady with blue hair a delightful afternoon. They both looked justifiably embarrassed. It made me happy, to see them fidget with shame—I am still a good Lutheran.

I drove to the lakefront and parked the car. I walked out on the bluff and gazed out at the lake, which was indeed aqua marine corduroy. It took my breath away. I died a little, but then was reborn. I had a better perspective, and a much more grateful attitude. I felt the despair lift, and I laughed at the silliness of my own self-pitying party. I was simply and suddenly aware of the many blessings this day had to bestow. I opened my soul and embraced it.

*   I wanted to go back and thank the blue-haired lady, but knew I already had by going to the lakefront and beholding the magical rippling colors of the water. She had ministered to the minister, and that was enough, and so it needed to be for me as well. In my own ministry, I, too, was enough. Maybe somebody did hear what I had to say today, or even received a message from a most gracious and generous God.*

A revelation is a mystery. It comes out of nowhere and everywhere at the same time. It may get noticed or missed in its entirety. It may alter a perspective or change an attitude, or be treated with complete disdain. Revelations can only be received. They are moments when we are suddenly transformed, brought back to life, and given a new sense of spirit. A revelation jars us loose and can blow us away.

A revelation is rightly called a shock to the system. It is a spiritual lightning bolt. When it strikes, we are suddenly freed of our loneliness, boredom, despair, or in my case, self-pity. It is not that we are made happy, or our cares and worries disappear, but we are now able to see and experience things in a whole new way.

Our kids need to understand how and why to look for a revelation. They need to know that they themselves will determine how receptive they are, and whether they are open to being embraced by a mysterious message. A sign, a symbol, God's signature scribbled across an ordinary day to day event, it is up to us to teach kids how to notice the revelatory moments of their lives.

"There can be no keener revelation of a society's soul
than the way in which it treats its children."
– Nelson Mandela

An Epiphany

"Gratitude bestows reverence, allowing us to encounter everyday epiphanies, those transcendent moments of awe that change forever how we experience life and the world."
— John Milton

An epiphany is in many respects like a revelation. The difference is subtle and spiritual. I personally believe that a revelation declares a message from God, an insight, an intuition, a sign inviting us to follow our spiritual instincts. An epiphany declares the presence of God. An epiphany is when we feel we are not only hearing from God, but also being granted an audience.

Epiphanies are spiritual events which deepen and tighten our bonds to God. A revelation will often change a perspective or attitude. An epiphany transforms a faith or a belief and frees us to feel a powerful intimacy with God. I believe a revelation informs us of the mind of God. An epiphany informs us of the wishes of God's heart.

She got up to go the bathroom. We had made love earlier that evening, and she seemed surprisingly restless. "I am pregnant," she said. I laughed and told her that might be nice. "I am pregnant," she repeated. I asked what made her think so. "I just know that I am, and I can't explain it, but I am. Trust me!"

She was. A month later the doctor informed her she was pregnant. She calmly nodded. Nine months later, our son Justin was born. She looked at me and said, "I told you." She had known in her heart. Her soul had been impregnated by an epiphany.

Many years later, she was in a comatose state, on her death bed. I asked her, "If you are still in there, please somehow let me know. I am here, and Justin will be fine, I know how to take good care of him. Just let me know you know." There was a pause, a puckering of her face, and then she blinked twenty consecutive times. Within minutes I was aware of the departure of her soul. It floated off like a butterfly, and I felt tears caress my cheeks just like the butterfly kisses she occasionally gave me before sleep.

I knew she was gone, but she would not be declared dead for another ten days. I just knew. I was grieving hard, but at peace. My wife of twenty-four years had departed days before her body could catch up. It felt like an epiphany to me. I could feel the presence of the Spirit. I sensed being touched in the deepest corners of my being.

A revelation and an epiphany are both transforming moments. When we are seized by the Spirit, or grasped by grace, we recognize that we are being changed in profound ways. We feel new. Some may call it being born again. It is a seismic shift. It is a homecoming for a soul long away.

Transforming moments touch us deeply. They move us not only to tears or to higher ground, but to a new beginning. In a spiritual way we are brought back to life. We are made whole and holy. We get the message. We see the point. Our soul settles and is satisfied. We know a peace which passes all understanding.

Once again, our children yearn to hear stories of epiphanies and revelations, times when life showed us a whole new way of being, a new path to follow, an intimacy with a God long thought to be distant. We need to share such magical miraculous moments with our young people, even if we question how crazy they might sound.

These are our miracle stories. Everyone has them. They are impossible to capture in words, but they demand expression. Miracles are transforming moments which defy logic or reason, and reorganize our lives in dramatic ways. Miracles alter the current of faith. The miraculous power of God is known in revelations, epiphanies, and snippets of grace. We cannot defend or explain or prove such experiences, but we are obligated to share them—they are good stories.

> "By an epiphany he meant a sudden spiritual manifestation, whether in the vulgarity of speech or of a gesture or memorable phrase of the mind itself. He believed it was for the man of letters to record these epiphanies with extreme care (saving them for later use, that is), seeing that they themselves are the most delicate and evanescent of moments."
> — James Joyce

A Glimpse of Grace

"The grace of God sets us free from a life of
perfection, performing, and pretending."
— Tullian Tchividjian

"The Grace of God means something like: Here is your life.
You might never have been, but you are because the party
wouldn't have been complete without you."
— Frederick Buechner

Let me be clear about something. A revelation, an epiphany, a transforming moment, a leap of faith, a glimpse of grace, are all so closely linked, the differences can only be called minimal, difficult to detect, and maybe even irrelevant to declare. I do so here only to offer up how I have personally experienced the movement of the Holy Spirit in my own life. I am fine with these terms being used interchangeably. I lift up the differences only as a means of distinguishing the spiritual impact such events have had on me—and this may indeed be limited only to me.

She was a friend and a parishioner. I knew her and trusted her. Her sister had been recently murdered by a stalker from her apartment complex, and I strongly suspected she was here to discuss the state of her grieving.

What she next told me left me empty and full, amazed and snide, and was overwhelming, both in its story and my desire to flee.

She woke on Saturday morning and began to sob. Her tears were torrents. She expressed that her grieving bordered on hysterics. It sounded to me as if it had long since crossed that border. She had gotten into her car, turned on some favorite music, and just started driving with no destination in mind. The weeping and wailing and gnashing of teeth continued for the duration of the drive.

Somewhere near Albany, a full four hours from home, she became aware she was driving to her parent's vacation home. It was a small cottage on a lake, and was a favorite memory for her, especially as it was where she got to play endlessly with her beloved sister. It still made no sense to be going there as it was certainly locked up in November, and the sun would soon be setting.

She arrived at the cottage and felt an urge to go inside. She looked under a rainbow-painted rock for the key, and lo and behold, it was still there, just it had been some thirty years ago. She entered the cottage, and her sobs were accompanied by inaudible screams. Her soul quaked.

She walked to the picture window in the living room, which overlooked the lake, and saw a burnt-orange sun settling on the lake's pink surface. She recalled a game her father had played with her sister and her. Each night of their vacation, her father would give a dime to the sister who saw the sun go down first. Neither sister ever figured out they each won every other night.

Her tears flowed, and she screamed out at the sunset, "You have even ruined sunsets. I can't even enjoy a damn sunset. How could you leave me like this?"

She then stated calmly and clearly that what she heard next was her sister's voice and wondrous laugh. "I am the sunset, you big dope! I am the sunset!" Then it was gone—as was a bulk of her grief.

She asked me in a matter of fact tone, "Well, Pastor Bill, what do you think?"

I really had nothing to say. Though my mind sought to provide insights and answers, I was left with a quivering glob of faith. My eyes were teary. I sighed deeply, and said, "I think you were paid a wonderful visit by your sister, and I envy you."

"Thank you, Pastor Bill, I think so, too. I know two things for sure. It was her voice and laugh, and I feel, well, utterly different. The sadness is still around, but not the anger or stress."

She got up to go, and we embraced. There was truly nothing left to say. I simply told her how grateful I was for her sharing her story with me. She said, "Somehow I knew you would be the one person who would not think I was nuts."

Of course, for the rest of the day I wondered if she was, but I kept coming back to something more basic. She had been visited by a spirit, and this was an experience I had heard a couple of dozen times in my forty-year ministry. I was just ticked off because nobody had visited me yet.

I refuse to debate anyone about the reality of visitations. It is a pure waste of time. It is a matter of faith—plain and simple. You either believe the story, or you don't. It is normal to question such a tale, and important to seriously ask if you trust the information being shared. For me, the bottom line is—I do not care.

Visitations are pure, raw, mysteries. They defy logic and rationale. They stretch the boundaries of the mind and break them down. They demand spiritual surrender. They are momentary and can never be fully grasped or held. They are like chasing after wind. So futile, until one day, one transforming moment, you notice you are carrying that wind under your arm and in your heart.

These visitation stories are sacred, holy, and shimmer with a longing which goes right to the heart of God. They are often not told because the risk of being mocked or ridiculed is way too high, and there is a genuine fear of contaminating the experience with doubt. It is like holding your breath when a bird lands in your palm. It will be gone soon enough. The moment demands to be swallowed whole.

My faith in visitations is simply based on their relative infrequency, simplicity, brevity, and the great difficulty those who have experienced one have in talking about it. There is a remarkable tension of fear and delighted awe in their voice. The sad part of such stories is how the impact fades over the years. Once the storyteller has departed, the thrill and delight of the story will soon wilt to a whimper. The story is one hundred percent dependent on the trustworthiness of the storyteller.

"All stories are true. But some of them never happened."
– James A. Owen, *The Search for the Red Dragon*

"There is no such thing as complete when it comes to stories. Stories are infinite. They are as infinite as worlds."
– Kelly Barnhill, *Iron Hearted Violet*

Dazzling Gradually

"The Truth must dazzle gradually / Or every man be blind."
— Emily Dickinson, "Tell all the truth but tell it slant—"

"Truth is tough. It will not break like a bubble, at a touch;
nay, you may kick it about all day like a football,
and it will be round and full at evening."
— Oliver Wendell Holmes, Sr., *The Professor at the Breakfast Table*

When you hear a story like the visitation of a sister who claims to be the sunset, one is left feeling childish and foolish while simultaneously most mature. The spiritual experiences we have—revelations, epiphanies, glimpses of God, miracles, visitations, whatever they may be called—are for *adults only*. A child may be enchanted by Santa Claus or believe a fairy tale can come true, but only mature adults receive messages from God. Maturity is the one requirement of the spiritual life. Maturity and spirituality are indeed, for the most part, one and the same.

A truly good story captures the truth. It lifts up a gospel truth. The truth of a really good story is not a fixed point. It is fluid, moving, growing, like a snowball rolling downhill. The truth, like us, must mature, or it will die. The truth, just like the soul, requires maturation as a means of being nourished. The truth must be kept from withering or rotting and is the responsibility of stories and storytellers.

The truth is a mystery. It is a quivering mass of holiness. It is the light. It is the Word of God. Engaging this mystery will mature us. The truth will lead us to an acceptance of our humanity and our divinity—such a mystery. The truth will bring us back to life by making us confront the reality of Death—how mysterious. The truth will defy us to lie, and keep us from living a lie. The truth will enable us to grow up, to become God's beloved children, cherished and adored at all times—what a delicious mystery to devour every day.

"As it unfolded the structure of story began to remind me of one of those Russian dolls that contain innumerable ever smaller dolls within. Step by step the narrative split into a thousand stories, as if it had entered a gallery of mirrors, its identity fragmented into endless reflections."
– Carlos Ruiz Zafon, *The Shadow of the Wind*

Let me tell you a simple, but lovely, true story.

I had taken my senior high youth group on a retreat weekend to an inn in Massachusetts. Confident of another great success, I was stunned by how poorly this one was going. The group fought over everything. Who rode in what car? Who would stay in what rooms? Would we eat Italian, Chinese, Mexican, or American? The actual planned discussions were flat and lifeless. They hated the movie we chose, and they endured bowling.

We were supposed to have a closing worship Sunday morning, but I decided to take a risk. I drove them to the Quabbin Reservoir, a spectacular setting of water and woods and wilderness. I led the group to the highest place in the park. I asked everyone to get out of the vans and gather on a hillside overlooking a vast stretch of sparkling water and hills lush with evergreens and lime laced spring trees.

I got the group to join hands in a large circle. They were scowling and muttering under their breath. Several asked me when we would be leaving. I next asked them to be seated, and asked one youth, Kelly, to sit in the middle of the circle. I told the group they each needed to share something about Kelly they liked, respected, enjoyed, or appreciated.

It started slowly, and I must admit, the adults took the lead, but soon each group member was offering a lovely and insightful comment about Kelly. Their comments were thoughtful, pretty accurate, and most of all, filled with genuine affection and compassion. Within minutes, tears were flowing, and would flow as we conducted the same exercise with and for every youth in the group.

It took over three hours to complete, and my butt went numb, but there was not a single complaint, and not one soul asked to leave.

We missed our ferry back to Long Island, but we caught the next one. The ride home was full of laughter and joy and true intimacy. Everything had changed—everything. A wretched weekend was now lifted up with good feelings, and it would always be remembered as such a wonderful time.

When this story is told, it will be all about the praise circle at the Quabbin—the rest of the weekend will be dismissed. There will be frustration in not being able to remember much of what was said. Still, the feeling will be captured. It felt like being held in the palm of God's hand. It was the embrace of grace, and it was so sweet.

It is such a mystery to me. How it is all in there. All the loving, forgiving, kindness, compassion, respect, genuine affection, and, well, just everything God hoped we might share in this life of ours. It just takes something to jar it loose. Something like directing a group of youth to sing each other's praises. It was so easy to ignite, and so ready to flow.

It is a mystery. Why do we wait and waste so much time and energy being shut up and down? It is right there—life is waiting for us to come home to our genuine selves and God. We have so much goodness and love to share, such kindness of spirit, and gentleness of soul. It is a mystery we do not spiritually explode—well, maybe we do, and maybe on a hillside in a circle, we did.

Story Starters

- When was the last time you got physically lost? How did you handle it? When were you most spiritually lost?
- How does mystery serve as a catalyst for spiritual maturation?
- When did you most powerfully experience the presence of God?
- Name a transforming moment you have recently experienced.
- Define an epiphany and a revelation. Is there a difference? What is it?

CHAPTER FIFTEEN

A Good Story Challenges Us to Embrace the Divine

"Love is an image of God, and not a lifeless image, but the living essence of the all divine nature which beams full of all goodness."
— Martin Luther

"God is like a mirror. The mirror never changes but everybody who looks at it sees something different."
— Rabbi Harold S. Kushner

"Science cannot answer the deepest questions. As soon as you ask why there is something instead of nothing, you have gone beyond science. I find it quite improbable that such order came out of chaos. There has to be some organizing principle. God to me is the explanation for the miracle of existence— why there is something instead of nothing.
— Cosmologist Allan R. Sandage

I am spiritually convinced we each possess a soul. The soul is the essence of our being. It is the place where contact with God was and is made. It is the dwelling for all which matters to us ultimately. It is the home of our wishes, dreams, hopes, ideals, and character. The soul is eternal, and this belief stems solely from my personal spiritual experiences.

I fully believe we all hold an idea of God in our souls. These ideas may be totally abstract or can be as concrete as a face-to-face encounter. For many of us, our idea of God is built upon experiences of the presence of God—as in nature or love or the raising of a child. For others, their idea may be the result of having felt deeply the absence of God—as in grief or a sense of abandonment or betrayal.

Each of us possesses a unique concept of a higher power. Our notions of God are the result of our history, intellect, family influences, life experiences, and how the Spirit is moving within us on any given day. Our ideas of God are always present, like the background noise of the universe.

Stories contain ideas of God. A good story expresses the heart of the soul. Good stories fill our minds with thoughts of God. A good story is a context conducive to the soul's maturation. Good stories enhance our compassion, encourage our courage, and call upon us to be creative. Good stories are loaded with characters and themes which speak of the will of God for our lives.

However, a good story does not preach, nor does it speak in the language of dogma. Stories are not out to prove the existence of God. Good stories simply offer hints and clues as to how and where to look for the presence of God. Stories do not defend a doctrine nor take up a cause or crusade. Good stories tell us how the Spirit infiltrates our days, inspires our hearts, infests our soul, and ignites our spirit.

I have come to the conclusion that the more detached from stories and storytellers our youth become, the more likely their faith in God will dwindle. A good story is a fertile field for the growth and development of a vibrant spiritual life. If our youth fail to hear good stories, they are losing out on an intimate conversation with God—one which is being conducted on a daily basis all over the world.

The Shame Game

"Unlike guilt, which is the feeling of doing something wrong,
shame is the feeling of being something wrong."
— Marilyn J. Sorensen

Too much of today's American religion is rooted in perfectionism and shame, and thus focused on what is wrong with us, while little attention is paid to what is right. Sadly, the Church is far too often in the habit of judging those who believe a different way. Far too many contemporary Christians have crafted a religion which bears little resemblance to an unconditionally loving Jesus. This is the religion of indoctrination. It is black and white, has all the answers, and rejects all who question or doubt its beliefs.

The good news of so many good stories is how they challenge this false notion. Good stories reveal the truth that we were not born into original sin, but are the spiritual heirs of original blessing. We are cherished and adored by a good and gracious God. Stories may reveal our flaws and failings, but they never do so in such a way as to invite feelings of hatred or the need for retribution. Stories are built upon a solid foundation of mercy. I have never read or heard a good story whose function it was to make anyone feel ashamed.

The divine is in nobody's possession. There are no omnipotent human beings. The Church must abandon its efforts to speak as if it possesses God. Our children need good stories from good adults who offer up their version and insights into the nature of God. We need to offer our ideas void of heavy doses of guilt, the abuse of shame, or the oppressive language of "should" and "must" and "have to."

I would much prefer hearing a teen tell me a story about how faith became real for them than to hear them recite a creed. I would have more respect for a youth performing an act of service than spouting memorized Bible verses. I am most impressed by the adolescent who seeks to understand, to look deep inside life, struggling to find meaning in his or her days, rather than to listen to a youth utter some religious formula which puts everything into one nice, neat tidy package.

A good story is never a nice, neat tidy package. It is a package which offers a messy gift. It is what is inside the package that matters and how it manages to change us, inspire us, and enables us to become better people. A good story offers us the gift of being in touch with our longings and yearnings and deepest desires, and this is never neat, ordered, or tidy. It may be harsh to call it a mess, but it is—life is messy, especially when the soul gets involved.

Shame is a slap to the soul for making a mess. Faith is a caress of the soul for cherishing the mess. Good stories are a celebration, and refuse to be laced with shame.

"Shame cannot survive being spoken...and being met with empathy."
– Brene Brown

The Color of Light

"Colors are the deeds of light, its deeds and sufferings."
— Johann Wolfgang Von Goethe

Religion has a compulsive appetite for black and white answers. The compulsively religious tend to declare their answers as truth and thereby expect them to be strictly adhered to. The net result is that religion has too often become a source of friction, division, hatred, and war.

Religion frequently promotes the notion of owning God, having God in one's hip pocket, or being able to speak for God. Religion paints God in black and white, with clear boundaries and borders, like a coloring book page. Religion too often states complex mysteries as if they were obvious facts.

Stories are never crafted in black and white. A good story is the color of light. The spectrum of color is vast and the hues infinite. Stories try to bring the truth to life, and this requires color. Life is simply not painted in black and white. It is never all that simple. Life's palette is as broad as God's mercy, and it's just as vibrant.

Stories do not attempt to capture God or the truth. Stories seek only to reveal the image of the divine. I am an avid reader, and I have read many sentences, paragraphs, full stories, even whole novels, which I have felt were divinely inspired. However, such divine inspiration does not eliminate the human hand of the author. Divinity does not devour humanity—it enhances it—and lifts the human soul up to the light.

Can a human soul be inspired by the divine? Yes, it can. Can a human soul explain the soul of God? No, it cannot, even in the Bible.

The soul sees in color. Stories are composed of light and shadow, and they can reveal rainbows. For those who seek contact with the divine, they must become artists of the soul. They will compose eternal stories which will last lifetimes. They will express the truth in poetry and myth and fairy tale—all excellent forms of telling a story. The good news of God's grace cannot be reproduced exactly in human language, but our words can offer guidance which points toward God.

Good stories are like steps up to higher ground. If we climb them, we will get a better view of ourselves, our lives, our God, and what matters most.

"The soul is dyed the color of its thoughts. Think only on those things that are in line with your principles and can bear the light of day. The content of your character is your choice. Day by day, what you do is who you become. Your integrity is your destiny—it is the light that guides your way."

— Heraclitus

Just a Myth

"I don't like the word 'allegorical,' I don't like the word 'symbolic'—
the word I really like is 'mythic,' and people always think that means
'full of lies,' whereas of course what it really means is 'full of truth
which cannot be told in any other way but a story.'"
– William Golding

It was time for Vacation Church School again, and as always, I was struck and disappointed by the limited nature of the curriculum. How many times had I taught the story of Moses in a basket, Noah's Ark, Jonah and the Whale, David and Goliath, *and* The Tower of Babel. *Though they are all good stories, well worth being repeated, even I had grown weary of their limited palette.*

It was Wednesday, and we were mobbed. We were a free summer babysitting service for exhausted mothers already sick of their children's summer vacation. I was making my rounds to the various classrooms, only to walk into a lively exchange between one of our teachers and a nine-year-old boy.

"Well, that never happened. There is no boat large enough to fit two of every species. I don't believe it. Maybe a couple hundred, but not every single species. That's nuts."

"Well, Chad, with God, all things are possible."

"No, it isn't. Otherwise they could do it again, and they can't, and so it never happened that way."

"Well, that is why we call it faith, Chad, because it means believing in things that are hard to believe."

"That isn't hard to believe, it is impossible!"

Though Sally, the fourth and fifth-grade teacher was doing an admirable job trying to answer the doubts of a very bright ten-year-old boy, I decided to intervene.

"Chad, what is a myth?"

"It is a lie, something that isn't true."

"Did you know that was not what a myth meant in Biblical times? It meant something quite the opposite. It meant trying to put into words something beyond words. It meant trying to capture the truth, even when the author knew it was impossible. It was like trying to hold water in your fist. A myth was the best attempt of a human being trying to express something which could never be fully captured in words."

"I don't get it."

"Chad, could you ever prove to us that you love your mother?"

"No...not really. But I could give an example."

"But that would not prove it, right?"

"Right."

"Why? Why can't you prove it?"

"Because, there aren't enough words."

"That is right, because there are not enough words. Human beings always fall short. This is why they often rely on stories to make their point. They are not trying to prove something, but they are trying to share what they believe. Chad, the story of Noah and the Ark *was a story of faith. It was a myth. It was a story meant to show just how much God loved everything in Creation. I think it did that. It may not be true, like a fact, but it sure does make a truthful point."*

"So, the story of Noah and the Ark *is a myth?"*

"Yes, but it is not a lie, it is just a wonderful effort to show God's deep

love for Creation in the face of a devastating flood. Does that make sense?"

"A little bit, I guess. Myths are a little bit fact, and a little bit story."

"Chad, I agree. It is a lovely story with a good message, and it sure does make a powerful point. And that is the point. The point it what makes the myth matter."

Sally came up to me at the end of the day and smiled and told me I had done a good job. I told her the same. She then told me to expect I would be hearing about calling the story of Noah's Ark *a myth, and I knew she was right. I wound up meeting with several parents and the Christian Education Committee twice over my scandalous response to Chad.*

How sad. Here is a bright young boy who was making perfect sense, and I was supposed to tell him he was wrong. Well, he was not wrong. He was right. What I tried to do was let him know there was a reason why such stories are shared in the Bible, and how important the points they make are.

Chad got it. Hopefully, someday the Church will also grow up, and celebrate stories of faith for what they truly are—an attempt to share a story about something too magnificent to put into words.

All good stories are made up of fact and fiction. Stories cannot be separated from the testimony of the storyteller. The storyteller is always editor, offering not only his or her version of events, but their own bias and perspective and colorful embellishments. It is never the intention of a good story to force someone into a way of seeing or thinking or believing.

Stories, like God, do not desire cloning, but rather attempt to inspire maturation. The Church must soon work itself out of the trap of insisting we all hear a story, even a Biblical one, in one particular way. That is not the way of faith, but the path of knowledge—the difference is huge.

Much of the Bible is myth and poetry and fairy tale. This does not mean it is false or fake or phony. It means mere words cannot contain the divine. The creators of myths and fairy tales understand they have a purpose other than being a historian. They are writing make believe—*trying to make us believe*. For example, a poet writes of a whipping wind scraping a face like a scalpel, not to depict the wind as a surgeon, but to enable us to actually feel that wind.

The Bible is not a reference book of religious answers, but a significant source of the spiritual life. The Bible is written in the language of eternity, in sighs and whispers and silence, and it shouts its truth from soul to soul. The Bible is not a history book, but the spiritual journal of a whole people—a diary of faith.

That is the point here. Good stories make good points and these points point to the presence of the divine. The point is not putting the divine in a box, or limiting God to the words of a creed, or reducing God to black and white dogmatic answers. The point is in pointing out how the divine paints our world and creates in the color of light.

You Shall Be as Gods

"Every human life is a reflection of divinity, and...every act of
injustice mars and defaces the image of God in man."
— Martin Luther King, Jr.

I recall being awed and overwhelmed at Seminary by the attention
paid to the notion of how humans shall be as gods. I heard sermons and
stories which spoke brilliantly of how we were created in the image of
God, and of Jesus telling us how we would do far greater things than
Him. I was stunned by the message that the Kingdom of God was in my
midst, and that I carried God in my heart.

I must admit, my childhood history in the Church had a completely
different focus. I was bombarded with the message of my badness, and
how far I fell short of what God had hoped. I clearly recall a male
Sunday School teacher who made me feel as if I were an inch shy of evil,
and who looked at me in such a way as to invoke disgust. Now, here at
Seminary, I was encountering fully, as if for the first time, the radical
message of grace.

I was taught how Jesus was the event of grace. Jesus brought grace
to Earth and life and each and every one of us. I was hearing of being a
beloved child of God and how I could make a significant difference. I was
being mentored in the words of unconditional love and mercy and with

the thrilling declaration of becoming new on a daily basis. I don't believe I ever felt born again, but I did find it all transformative.

Good stories are riddled by grace. They are not like a Hallmark Card or movie, which, by the way, would not be a bad thing, but good stories take on an even greater depth, are more morally rigorous, and call us to radical changes. Good stories call us not only to be our best, but to bring out the best in others, to be rigorously honest and robustly merciful, to love when we are least inclined, to love those who do not even deserve our attention, and to create the Kingdom of God on this good Earth in this good time.

Good stories, in the spirit of the Creator, step back and boldly announce, "And this too is good!" We are good. Our lives are good. This Earth is good. Our neighbors are good. Our families and our friends are good. God is so good. This is the good news calling us to the genuine good life, and this is when we begin to encounter the divine on a daily basis.

"Jesus was not a theologian. He was a God who told stories."
— Madeleine L'Engle, *Walking on Water: Reflections on Faith and Art*

Co-Creators

"Everybody born comes from the Creator trailing
wisps of glory. We come from the Creator with creativity.
I think that each one of is born with creativity."
— Maya Angelou

True creativity is not the same thing as being artsy-crafty. True creativity is a dynamic process which seeks to resolve a conflict. Good stories are acts of creation. A story which will move us or touch our hearts is never without conflict. Sadness, anger, loss, grief, being lost, feeling hopeless, experiencing betrayal, fear, anxiety, having no friends, or thinking of oneself as a failure, being unable to love or forgive, or lacking in faith or courage—these are the kinds of conflicts with which good stories wrestle.

The creative process involves a moment of insight—a spark of inspiration—followed by a time of wrestling with the issue, an interlude for quiet and isolated reflection, a breakthrough, a resolution, and an application. In a spiritual way, this process is quite parallel to giving birth. From the time of heated coupling, to the sharing of seed, a dynamic struggle of sperm and egg, the incubation of pregnancy, and the sharp sudden pains of labor, to the actual giving of birth—birth is a suitable paradigm for all creativity.

I find stories offer us images of human beings becoming co-creators with God. These tales and fairy tales speak to us about how humanity reveals the image of the divine by not only solving the conflicts we face, but by doing and being people who promote the continuation of life. As a co-creator, we vow to preserve and protect the Creation as a whole, and our stories display our human effort to do so. By creating hope and happiness, resolving guilt and grief, healing wounds and diseases, and helping the world make peace with itself, we indeed have taken on a most godly function.

Some of these stories are spellbinding in their acts of courage and the surrendering of self on someone else's behalf, while others are far smaller and simpler, but no less significant, which tell of transforming acts of justice, kindness, and compassion. A majority of these stories speak of human being helping human being, and yet, many are of humanity showing mercy to the Earth and the universe and life and yes, God—as we understand God.

Grafting on Grace

"Forgiveness is the grace by which you enable the other person
to get up and get up with dignity anew."
— Desmond Tutu

When I was a senior at Princeton Theological Seminary, I found myself truly struggling to find a theme for my senior thesis. Owing to my well acknowledged grandiosity, I fueled the issue by wanting to write the best senior thesis ever written—which puts a damper on creativity.

On a snowy Sunday afternoon, I was studying for Dr. Beker's class on the Pauline epistles. Never a big fan of Paul, I had so much respect for the wildly spiritual Beker, so I decided to dive into the material. I was reading Paul's letter to the Colossians, and the church in Colossae, when I came upon the following lines:

"As God's chosen ones, holy and beloved, clothe yourselves with compassion, kindness, humility, meekness, and patience. Bear with one another and, if anyone has a complaint against another, forgive each other; just as the Lord has forgiven you, so you must also forgive. Above all, clothe yourselves with love, which binds everything in perfect harmony. And let the peace of Christ rule in your hearts, to which indeed you were called in the one body. And be thankful. Let the word of Christ dwell in you richly; teach and admonish one another in all wisdom; and with gratitude in your hearts sing psalms, hymns, and spiritual songs to God. And whatever you do, in word or deed, do everything in the name of the Lord Jesus, giving thanks to God the Parent through him" (Colossians 3:12-17).

I had an epiphany that day—a spiritual revelation.

First, I was captured by being called chosen, holy, and beloved. The power of the grace declared in that salutation really hit me. Second, the word "clothe" flashed at me like a neon sign. Compassion, kindness, humility, meekness, and patience, were not always within me, but could be worn by me. It was not up to me to be perfect, but it was my choice on whether or not I would put Christ on and wear him like a cloak. Lastly, I was struck by the admonition to once again see love and mercy as the foundations of the Christian life, and there was the third—be grateful.

In modern culture, being a "put-on" is the equivalent of being a phony. In my eyes, and as my thesis, being a "put-on"—when what we are putting on is God—is the essence of all that is genuine. What a great gift to be able to graft grace onto our lives. These grafts always take. We are assured when we make the effort to cloak ourselves in God, we will witness the divine taking shape within and upon us. We will grow in grace, and grace will grow on and in us.

"Everyone has a spirit that can be refined, a body that can be trained in some manner, a suitable path to follow. You are here to realize your inner divinity and manifest your innate enlightenment."
– Morihei Ueshiba

Note the Divine

Justin was three years old. He was a bundle of electric energy. When he was awake, he was on the go. This was always true, unless he was sicker than a dog.

We had come to Grandma and Grandpa's for one of our final visits before moving to Long Island, where Christine had been called to serve the Old Whaler's Church. My folks were heartbroken over our departure and could not even speak of the loss of their Thursdays with Justin. Each week they had Justin for the whole day, as well as overnight, his outing completed with breakfast with Grandpa.

Grandpa was seated in his rocking chair and smoking his pipe. His eyes were teary, and his silence was screaming his sadness out loud. Justin was playing with his He-Man figurines, and Grandma had made a pillow fort in which they had played all morning. Justin called Grandpa to come over to the fort and help battle the enemy. My father wept and did not come. Justin noticed.

Justin left Grandma and the fort and toddled over to his Grandfather, then he crawled up in his lap. He then took one of my dad's many extra pipes and proceeded to pretend he was smoking and rocking with Grandpa. He stayed there for a full hour. As a parent and a son, it felt like a miracle.

Grandma and I were weeping. How did Justin know? How did the boy of mayhem and energy choose to sit still for an hour and rock? He had never done anything remotely like this before.

Justin eventually got up to leave and gave Grandpa a kiss and a pat on the cheek. At that moment, I no longer questioned what was happening, but simply believed it had been a moment of experiencing the divine. I took note of it. I paid attention. I felt healed and whole. I felt transformed.

These moments fill our days. Chips and slices of time soaked in God's presence, or which reflect God's will or love or mercy, or all three. These are morsels which lift up before us what is worthy of being called divine. These gracious Godly minutes are the stuff of good stories. That is our job, calling, mission, hope—to record those times when we were blown away by the presence of God. Again, remember, words will never recapture the full moment, but they are always worth the effort and the sharing.

Behold

"I existed from all eternity and, behold, I am here;
and I shall exist till the end of time, for my being has no end."
– Kahlil Gibran

Behold. What an old and wondrous word. A concept steeped in the tradition of reverence and awe. It is an idea which expresses our capacity to be held by the divine, and to receive the embrace of grace. It is the notion of our ability to grasp grace, and to hold the divine in our hearts and souls and even hands.

Good stories, at their core, their spiritual center, ask us to behold the divine. Every good story is celebrating the sweet goodness of life, and seeking to reveal the beauty even in the midst of great ugliness. Good stories offer up a vision of how God thinks, feels, believes. They invite us to behold the wisdom of God's presence.

Good stories poke and prod and push us toward the truth. They impart messages of eternal value and worth. They seek to establish conviction in us, the determination to build God's Kingdom in the here and now. Good stories, stories of mercy, extravagant love, kindness, humility, generosity, moral courage, determination, the actualization of dreams, the freedom from fear, the transforming powers of faith, are all grounded in beholding the divine in our lives.

Behold—stop. Behold—look. Behold—listen. Behold—notice. Behold—pay attention. Behold—experience the grip of grace. Behold—grasp after Grace. Behold—be ready to receive. Behold—be open in heart and mind and spirit. Behold—let God come in.

This is the glue which unites all good stories together. It is the unity found in the theme of calling us to behold. It is the harmony fostered by awed reverence, and beholding the love and mercy of God.

> "You become what you behold."
> – William Blake

Story Starters

- Is there someplace or someone or someway, which inspires you to consistently experience the presence of God?
- For what have you been made to feel ashamed? What was the role of shame within your family?
- Which stories have served to make you believe?
- How is the Kingdom found in your midst? How does being a co-creator with God show itself in your daily life?
- How would you like to graft God onto yourself at this moment in time?

THE CONCLUSION

Stop for a Good Story

"Carve your name on hearts, not tombstones. A legacy etched into the minds of others and the stories they share about you."
– Shannon L. Alder

I think of this book as a plea. I feel a true prophetic calling in my message here. It is a message I consider to be urgent, apparent, rampant, and threatening. The overwhelming of our children's souls by modern technology, and the subsequent loss of stories and storytellers, is an alarming trend. We have not even begun to adequately consider just how dangerous this phenomenon may be to their lives and to the spiritual condition of our culture.

I know that many of my readers will still be asking the question, "How do we get our kids back into stories and storytelling? How do we make it happen?" I wish there was a formula or a gimmick that works, or some secret I could bestow. There are none. There is simply learning to pay close attention to the stories being told in our lives, within our families and friendships, and recorded in our personal histories. We adults have to become better story collectors and educators, and yes, also good storytellers.

We must remember some basic spiritual facts about gathering stories. Stories take time to tell and hear. Stories require absolute quiet and stillness to be truly enjoyed and heard. Stories, the truly good ones, speak about subjects that matter eternally and to everyone. Good stories need good storytellers, and we need to find them. Almost every family has one or two. Who are they in your family? Good stories demand that we stop and savor.

It is important for us to begin to listen to our bodies and hearts and minds and souls as we seek to become more skilled in the art of storytelling. Our spirits will often tell us a truly good story is being told, heard, witnessed, experienced, or lived. When we are moved to tears, when we get a lump in the throat, when we get a shiver up and down the spine, when we are blown away, when we are left dumbstruck, when we get gooseflesh, when butterflies swarm inside our stomachs, when we are in awe, when we know love or mercy or hope, when we take a leap of faith, or jump for joy, when we sense we are being transformed, born again, or completely renewed, when we die laughing, but do not die and when we come to our senses, become wise, or "feel" the presence of God. Our beings will tell us when good stories are nearby, hovering about us, and looking for a soul upon which to land.

It is time for us to step up to the plate for our kids, and tell them the unpopular truth—technology is potentially addictive, compulsive, disturbing in its capacity to alienate the soul, and destructive of so much that makes us wonderfully human. Technology can be quite corrosive to our compassion, kindness, mercy, tenderness, tolerance, and genuine goodness. The good life spawned by technology has little to do with goodness.

Is this book anti-technology? No, but it does promote the honest labelling of technology, and admitting to ourselves and our kids the glaring dangers of technological gadgetry. We cannot hide our heads in the sand and continue to pretend that technology is inherently positive or productive. We cannot keep claiming technology as the cornerstone of progress without first answering the questions, "To what and where and why are we progressing?"

We must claim and name the numerous threats to the soul fostered by an out of control technology. I don't believe we need to produce more surveys and statistics to acknowledge what we already know to be true— our kids spend way too much time fixated on technology. We all see it. We all experience it. It is routinely displayed in movies, books, and magazines, and we hear it constantly in teen conversation.

We can say NO to technology. We can limit the amount of time our kids spend on its usage. We can talk openly about its addictive properties and help our kids understand just how compulsive it can be.

We must begin to better mentor our kids on the vital importance of developing a deep and full spiritual life—which may or may not be religious. Our children need us to decide to become adults who are mature, hopeful, joyful, playful, creative, and lead a balanced and full life. Our kids need to know that adulthood is not some dizzying rat race held for soulless automatons. They need us to live as if they were indeed created in the image of God.

This is not an easy sell in America—asking folks to slow down, be quiet, take some time to be still, and open up their minds and hearts to a whole new way of living. Good stories are out there screaming about hope and joy and love and mercy and compassion and respect and courage and conviction, and there just not much of an audience. This book is asking that we become that audience.

We must also bring our kids to the show. Let them learn about the magical art of stories and storytelling. How stories can enchant and entertain, teach and tutor, guide and direct the human soul into having a life which is full of deep satisfaction, meaning, and worth. We are being invited to Heaven for a time, here and now, in our midst, by stories which are eternal and connect with other souls that are equally so.

I hope you have heard within these pages the stories calling out to you, offering you real intimacy and genuine hope, and asking to be your lifelong friend. Stories go deep, and are never shallow or trite. Stories are to be savored and not devoured. Stories are slow and have no fascination with speed. Stories are universal and have no select listeners. Stories are unafraid of addressing mysteries, the dark side, even the ugly side, and of course, focus heavily on the human side. Stories lack fear and are written out of faith in us, life, and God.

Good stories are all about goodness and a genuine good life. Good stories expect grace and mercy and respect. Good stories create meaning and hope and joy and freedom and a wild embrace of living on God's terms, not our own. Good stories celebrate that we are not in charge or in control, and so, the mantra of a good story is to surrender, to claim our powerlessness, to walk the walk and quit talking.

A truly good story is rigorously honest and always heading for higher ground. The view from this higher ground is of a Kingdom being built by human hands and hearts and voices. It is a place where there are no first and third worlds, no gaps between rich and poor, and no divisions of races and religions. It is what was once called Paradise.

I cannot give you these stories. I cannot offer you a map nor create for you the scenic overlooks along the way. I can only encourage you to have the courage to start looking and listening and feeling and seeking for the stories of your life.

I beg you to do so for your children, or grandchildren, and for all the good kids of this good earth. We owe them the truth, the gospel truth, and that is to be found in the stories of our lives. I call upon you, and challenge you, and hope I have somehow inspired you, to realize that our kids' souls are at risk, and how much they deserve to hear all about ordinary lives which reveal just how beautiful life can be.

Our kids need leadership and inspiration, and they need mature adults offering them concrete hope. They need to know we do know what matters. We understand what makes life worth the living. It is not rocket science. It is to be found in loving extravagantly and without conditions and to forgive everyone everything. We must live out what we know is the truth. We have to find the courage to no longer passively accept the lies being offered up as mandates by our culture.

We have to say *enough* to technology, and get it back under control. If it is to have a place in our kids' lives, it must be behind all the good stories out there in the wilderness crying to be heard.

"People who care nothing for their country's stories and song,' he said, 'are like people without a past— without memory—they are half people."
– Alasdair Gray, Poor Things

Story Starters

Build or buy a wooden chest. Keep story starters inside. Photos. Clippings. Poems. Notes. Invitations. Essays. Written stories. Keepsake items. Tokens of remembrance. Hold a yearly gathering to open the chest, and share a few good stories inspired by the contents of the chest.

APPENDIX

I have saved the following data until now, as I did not want this to be another book that scares parents to death. I want this book to offer hope. I want this book to inspire. I firmly believe that in sharing life's many sacred stories we have a vital resource for the nourishment of the soul as well as a powerful means of helping our kids become the best they can be—and who God dreamed them to be.

I am presenting a small but wide sampling of statistical information here, and it does carry a core message, which is the tremendous difficulty our children are having growing up in this culture. My call for storytelling to help feed the young soul has been deeply influenced by the "bad news" you will read about here—it is a formidable foe we are up against.

This is not an attempt to blame technology for all adolescent issues in America, but it is a call to be aware of the intimate connection between a weak soul and quite dangerous behavior. Remember, this is just a sampling, and there are loads of articles and statistical data on the addictive use of technology by our children—and by us, their role models. Read up and be informed on how big a problem this is becoming and how rapidly our youth are being swept away by a virtual tsunami of personal technology.

Again, the statistics offered here on some of the major issues of adolescence only serves to highlight the enormous need for helping our young mature their souls—as well as a challenge to us to lead the way.

From The International Center for Media and Public Agenda (ICMPA):

A majority of kids and teens spend about 75% of their waking lives attached to a screen of some sort.

A study asked 1,000 students in ten countries on five continents to quit using technology and media for just *one* day. Here are some of the findings and the kids' responses:

1. Students used the term "addiction" when describing their dependence on media.

2. A vast majority of students <u>failed to unplug for even one day</u>, admitting to the researchers that they gave in before twenty-four hours had passed.

3. Most students said they felt lost, alone, and <u>excessively lonely</u> when their screens were taken from them.

4. Students had zero ideas about <u>how to fill up their empty hours</u> without media and screens. They spoke of being excessively bored.

5. Tech is an escape mechanism more so than an enjoyment.

From Helpguide.org:

"While time spent online can be hugely productive, compulsive Internet use can interfere with daily life, work, and relationships. When you feel more comfortable with your online friends than your real ones, or you can't stop yourself from playing games, gambling, or compulsively checking your smartphone, tablet, or other mobile device—even when it is has negative consequences in your life—then you may be using the Internet too much."

"Many people turn to the Internet in order to manage unpleasant feelings such as stress, loneliness, depression, and anxiety. When you have a bad day and are looking for a way to escape your problems or to quickly relieve stress or self-soothe, the Internet can be an easily accessible outlet. Losing yourself online can temporarily make feelings such as loneliness, stress, anxiety, depression, and boredom evaporate into thin air. As much comfort as the Internet can provide, though, it's important to remember that there are healthier (and more effective) ways to keep difficult feelings in check. These may include exercising, meditating, and practicing simple relaxation techniques."

"While online pornography and cybersex addictions are types of sexual addiction, special challenges on the Internet include its relative anonymity and ease of access. It's easy to spend hours on the Internet in the privacy of your own home and engage in fantasies impossible in real life."

From http://teendrugabuse.us:

"Forty percent of those who start drinking at age thirteen or younger developed alcohol dependence later in life. Ten percent of teens who began drinking after the age of seventeen developed dependence."

"Alcohol kills six and a half times more teenagers than all other illicit drugs combined."

"Teenagers whose parents talk to them on a regular basis about the dangers of drug use are 42% less likely to use drugs than those whose parents don't."

From DoSomething.org:

"More teens die from prescription drugs than heroin/cocaine combined."

"The United States represents 5% of the world's population and 75% of prescription drugs taken. Sixty percent of teens who abuse prescription drugs get them free from friends and relatives."

"About 50% of high school seniors do not think it's harmful to try crack or cocaine once or twice, and 40% believe it's not harmful to use heroin once or twice."

From SADD:

"In 2009, 11.1% of youth in grades 9-12 reported being in a physical fight."

"Nearly 8% of students reported being threatened or injured with a weapon on school property at least one time during the past year."

"One in five students reported being bullied on school property during the past year."

"Juveniles accounted for 16% of all violent crime arrests and 26% of all property crime arrests in 2008."

"In 2009, 46% of high school students had sexual intercourse and 13.8% had four or more sex partners during their life. Prior to sexual activity, 21.6% drank alcohol or used drugs. Only 38.9% used a condom."

"Each year, approximately 19 million new STD infections occur, and almost half of them are among youth ages 15-24."

"The most common reasons youth receive mental health services are feeling depressed (50%), problems at home/family (28.8%), breaking rules or "acting out" (25.1%), and suicidal thoughts or attempts (20.2%)."

From National Center for Children in Poverty:

"Approximately 20% of adolescents have a diagnosable mental health disorder."

"Many mental health disorders first present during adolescence."

"Between 20% to 30% of adolescents have one major depressive episode before they reach adulthood."

"An estimated 67% to 70% of youth in the juvenile justice system have a diagnosable mental health disorder."

"Suicide is the third leading cause of death in adolescents and young adults."

"Between 500,000 and one million young people aged 15 to 24 attempt suicide each year."

"Older adolescents (aged 15-19) are at an increased risk for suicide (7.31/100,000)."

"Rates of serious mental health disorders among homeless youth range from 19% to 50%."

From ABC News:

"At age fourteen or fifteen, a perfect storm of surging hormones, immature brains and unfamiliar emotions drive nearly one in twelve teens to deliberately hurt themselves, most often by cutting or burning their own flesh, or by trying to hang, electrocute, drown, or suffocate themselves."

"Self-harm is common, reported by about 8% percent of fourteen to nineteen-year olds.

Yes, we could go on and on and on here and bury ourselves in alarming horrible news. Suffice it to say, there is a real wake-up call in this avalanche of data. We must be mature adults who are alert and awake to the world in which our children live and the issues they face on a daily basis. Since technology grows and transforms at such a ridiculous pace, we are also being asked to become even more acutely aware of our responsibility to stay informed.

We caring and compassionate adults are more than equipped to create some hope for our children and to protect their souls, as well inspire their spiritual maturation. We can, and will do it, by being adults in possession of vibrant and vital souls.

"Maybe stories are just data with a soul."
— Brene Brown